J. G. Wood

Routledge's Picture Book of Birds

J. G. Wood

Routledge's Picture Book of Birds

ISBN/EAN: 9783337138448

Printed in Europe, USA, Canada, Australia, Japan

Cover: Foto ©ninafisch / pixelio.de

More available books at **www.hansebooks.com**

BEWICK'S SWAN.—*Cygnus minor.*   WHISTLING SWAN.—*Cygnus ferus.*   MUTE SWAN.—*Cygnus olor.*

ROUTLEDGE'S
PICTURE BOOK

OF

BIRDS

BY

THE REV. J. G. WOOD, M.A., F.L.S.

Author of the "Illustrated Natural History"

WITH TWO HUNDRED AND FORTY-TWO ILLUSTRATIONS BY WOLF, ZWECKER, WEIR, COLEMAN, ETC.
ENGRAVED BY THE BROTHERS DALZIEL.

LONDON
GEORGE ROUTLEDGE AND SONS
THE BROADWAY, LUDGATE
NEW YORK: 416 BROOME STREET
1878

PREFACE.

In the pages of a well-known Latin poet, there is a remark to the effect that words spoken to the ear alone often are forgotten, but that they retain their hold if impressed upon the memory by the aid of the eye.

On this principle this little work has been undertaken, greater stress being laid upon the illustrations than on the description. In the letter-press will, however, be found sufficient information to give the name and general habits of each bird, together with the country which it inhabits.

In so small a work it is manifestly impossible to give more than a few out of the vast multitudes of the feathered tribes, or to devote much space to describing the specimens which have been selected. The reader will, however, find that those birds have been chosen which serve as the types of the various groups into which the Birds have been divided by zoologists, and that almost every important group is represented by one or more examples.

The arrangement which has been followed is that of the British Museum; and the young reader will find that the book will act as a guide to that magnificent collection, and enable him to attain a tolerably comprehensive view of the Birds therein placed.

As the work is not of a scientific character, the technical descriptions of the structure have been intentionally omitted. The reader will, however, find such information in my larger "Illustrated Natural History," to which he is referred for further descriptions and a much more comprehensive view of Birds.

London,
        October, 1861.

CONTENTS.

Accentor, 91.
Adjutant, 224.
Albatros, Wandering, 243.
Apteryx, 213.
Aratoo, Goliath, 171.
Barbet, Hairy-breasted, 177.
" White-faced, 50.
Bee-eater, 57.
" Azure-throated, 58.
Bell Bird, 114.
Bittern, 221.
Blackbird, 105.
" Savannah, 183.
Bower Bird, Spotted, 137.
Breve, Giant, 99.
Bullfinch, 154.
Bunting, Yellow, 152.
Bustard, Great, 214.
Buzzard, 16.
" Turkey, 4.
Campanero, 114.
Canary Bird, 149.
Capercaillie, 207.
Caracara, Southern, 14.
Cariama, 217.
Cassowary, 212.
Chaffinch, 147.
Channel-bill, 184.
Chiff-chaff, 85.
Chough, 133.
Cissa, Hunting, 122.
Cock of the Rock, 113.
Cockatoo, Great White, 172.
" Leadbeater's, 174.
" Sulphur-crested, 173.
Coly, Senegal, 156.
Comet, Sappho, 73.
Condor, 2.
Coquette, Spangled, 72.
Cormorant, 247.
" Crested, 247.
Corncrake, 232.
Crane, 218.
" Crowned, 219.
" Demoiselle, 219.
Creeper, Common-Tree, 78.
" Curved-billed, 77.
Crossbill, 155.

Crow, 125.
" Bald Fruit, 131.
" Great-billed, 128.
" Piping, 119.
Cuckoo, 185.
" Pheasant, 182
Curassow, crested, 194.
Curlew, 227.
" Pigmy, 228.
Dacelo, Buff, 52.
Dicrurus, Great, 116.
Dipper, 100.
Diver, Great Northern, 239.
Dodo, 193.
Dotterel, 215.
Dove, Ring, 187.
" Stock, 187.
" Turtle, 190.
Duck, Eider, 238.
" Mandarin, 236
Dunlin, 228.
Eagle, Bald, 13.
" Bold, 8.
" Cinereous, 12.
" Crested, 10.
" Golden, 7.
" Harpy, 10.
" Sea, 12.
" White-headed, 13.
" White-tailed, 12.
Egret, 221.
Emeu, 211.
Falcon, Laughing, 9.
" Peregrine, 20.
" Swallow-tailed, 18.
Fantail, White-shafted, 110.
Fieldfare, 103.
Finches, 146.
Flamingo, 233.
Flycatcher, Pied, 111.
" Spotted, 111.
Friar Bird, 67.
Gannet, 246.
Goat Sucker, European, 36.
" Leona, 38.
" Long-tailed, 37.
" Trinidad, 35.
Goldfinch, 147.

Goose, Bean, 234.
" Grey-lag, 234.
" Solan, 246.
Goshawk, 23.
Grebe, Eared, 240.
" Great Crested, 240.
Greenfinch, 148.
Grosbeak, 143.
" Black and Yellow, 144.
Grouse, Ruffed, 208.
Guinea Fowl, 204.
Gull, Black-backed, 245.
Gull, Common, 245.
" Kittiwake, 245.
" Skua, 245.
Harrier, Hen, 26.
" Jardines, 27.
Hawfinch, 143.
Hawk, Sparrow, 24.
Heron, 221.
Hoatzin, 159.
Honey-Eater, Garrulous, 65.
Honey Guide, Great, 181.
" Sucker, Blue-headed, 64.
Hoopoe, 62.
Hornbill, Crested, 161.
" Rhinoceros, 161.
" Two-horned, 161.
" White-crested, 161.
" Woodpecker, 161.
Humming-bird, Hermit, Salle's, 70.
" Ruby, and Topaz 74.
" Sickle-bill, 71.
" Snow-cap, 72.
" Vervain, 75.
" White-Booted, Racket-tail, 69.
Ibis, Sacred, 226.
" Glossy, 226.
Jacamar, Green, 56.
" Paradise, 56.
Jacana, 230.
Jackass, Laughing, 51.
Jackdaw, 127.
Jay, 120.
" Blue, 121.
Jerfalcon, 19.

CONTENTS.

Kestrel, 22.
King Bird, 109.
Kingfisher, 55.
   „   Australian, 53.
   „   Spotted, 54.
Kite, 17.
   „   Brazilian, 15.
Knot, 228.
Lammergeyer, 1.
Landrail, 232.
Lark, Sky, 153.
Linnet, 148.
Lorrikeet, Scaly-breasted, 167.
Love-bird, 170.
Lyre-bird, 80.
Macaw, Blue and Yellow, 168.
Magpie, 180.
Mallard, 237.
Martin, Fairy, 43.
   „   House, 44.
Merlin, 21.
Mocking Bird, 101.
Motmot, Brazilian, 46.
Neomorpha, 60.
Nightingale, 87.
Nightjar, 36.
Nutcracker, 129.
Nuthatch, 79.
Oriole, Baltimore, 141.
   „   Golden, 108.
   „   Orchard, 140.
Ostrich, 210.
Osprey, 11.
Ousel, Ring, 104.
Oven Bird, 76.
Owl, Barn, 34.
   „   Burrowing, 30.
   „   Canada, 28.
   „   Coquimbo, 30.
   „   Long-eared, 33.
   „   Snowy, 29.
   „   Tengmalm's, 31.
   „   Virginian-eared, 32.
   „   White, 34.
Paradise Bird, Emerald, 135.
   „   Golden, 136.
   „   King, 135.
Parrakeet, Blue-banded Grass, 166.
   „   Cockatoo, 163.
   „   Ground, 165.
   „   Rose Hill, 164.
Parrot, Grey, 169.
   „   Owl, 176.
   „   Philip Island, 175.

Parson Bird, 66.
Partridge, 205.
Pastor, Rose-coloured, 138.
Peacock, 197.
Pelican, 248.
Penguin, King, 242.
Pettichaps, Lesser, 85.
Pheasant, 198.
   „   Golden, 199.
   „   Silver, 199.
Pie, Wandering, 123.
Pigeon, Crowned, 191.
   „   Domestic, 188.
   „   Passenger, 186.
   „   Tooth-billed, 192.
   „   Topknot, 189.
Pipit, Meadow, 98.
   „   Tree, 98.
Plantain-eater, Blue, 158.
Plover, Golden, 215.
   „   Kentish, 215.
Plume Bird, Twelve-thread, 61.
Poë Bird, 66.
Poultry, Domestic, 201.
Puffin, 241.
Quail, 206.
Rail, Water, 232.
Raven, 124.
Redbreast, 90.
Redstart, 89.
Rifle Bird, 59.
Roller, Garrulous, 45.
Rook, 126.
Screamer, Crested, 231.
   „   Horned, 231.
Secretary Bird, 25.
Sheath-bill, White, 209.
Shrike, Great Grey, 117.
   „   Piping Crow, 119.
   „   Vigor's Bush, 118.
Skylark, 153.
Snipe, Common, 229.
   „   Jack, 229.
Sparrow, 151.
   „   Hedge, 91.
   „   Tree, 151.
Spoonbill, 222.
Starling, Common, 139.
Stint, Temmink's, 228.
Stonechat, 88.
Stork, 223.
   „   Whale-headed, 225.
Sun-bird, Fiery-tailed, 63.
Swallow, 42.
   „   Australian, Needle-tailed, 39.

Swallow, Esculent, 41.
   „   Wood, 115.
Swan, Bewick's, *Front*.
   „   Black, 235.
   „   Mute, *Front*.
   „   Whistling, *Front*.
Swift, 40.
Tailor Bird, 82.
Tanager, Scarlet, 145.
Thrush, Missel, 102.
   „   Song, 106.
   „   Spotted Ground, 107.
Titmouse, Blue, 93.
   „   Great, 92.
   „   Long-tailed, 95.
   „   Rufous-bellied, 94.
   „   Yellow-cheeked, 94.
Tody, King, 112.
Toucan, 162.
Touraco, White-crested, 157.
Trogon, Beautiful, 49.
   „   Cuba, 48.
   „   Malabar, 48.
   „   Massena's, 47.
   „   Mexican, 47.
Trumpeter, Golden Breasted, 217
Turkey, 202.
   „   Brush, 195.
   „   Honduras, 203.
Turnstone, 216.
Umbrella Bird, 132.
Vulture, Bearded, 1.
   „   Carrion, 4.
   „   Egyptian, 6.
   „   Griffin, 5.
   „   King, 3.
Wagtails, 96.
   „   Pied, 97.
   „   Yellow, 97.
Wandering Pie, 123.
Warbler, Blackcap, 86.
   „   Willow, 85.
Wattle Bird, Brush, 68.
Weaver Bird, Rufous-necked, 142.
Whimbrel, 227.
Whinchat, 88.
Woodpecker, Spotted, 178.
   „   Ivory-billed, 179.
Woodstar, Yarrell's, 73.
Wren, 81.
   „   Emeu, 83.
   „   Fire-crested, 84.
   „   Golden-crested, 84.
   „   Willow, 85.
Wryneck, 180.
Yellow-ammer, 152.

LAMMERGEYER.—*Gypaëtus barbatus.*

The Bearded Vulture, or Lammergeyer, lives in the rocky parts of South Europe and Western Asia. It eats dead animals, rats, mice, and hares, and sometimes steals lambs from the fold. Sometimes it kills the Chamois Goat by knocking it off the rock with its long wings. It is called the Bearded Vulture, on account of the long tufts of black hair-like feathers which fall from the nostrils and beneath the beak. The bird is greyish brown, dotted with white above, and white below.

CONDOR.—*Sarcorhamphus Gryphus.*

The Condor is an enormous bird, living in America, in the Andes, and ascends to the tops of the highest mountains. Two Condors will sometimes attack a Cow or a Llama, and kill it with their strong beaks and claws. It is very strong, and cannot easily be killed. The Indians catch these birds with lassos, while they are sitting gorged with food. The colour of the full-grown Condor is deep blackish grey.

KING VULTURE.—*Sarcorhamphus Papa.*

The King Vulture lives in the hottest parts of America. It is called the King of the Vultures because it is large and strong, and will not allow the common Vultures to begin a meal until it has satisfied its own hunger. Its head is beautifully coloured with scarlet, yellow, and blue. It lives in the forests, and is usually seen near swamps and marshes, where it can find plenty of dead creatures. It is a handsome bird, with satiny-white back, deep black wings, and brightly coloured head.

TURKEY BUZZARD.—*Catharista Aura.*

The Turkey Buzzard, or Carrion Vulture, is another American bird, and is very useful in eating animals which are found dead and dying, or which are killed by hunters, and left on the ground after the hunters have finished their meal. Its name of Turkey Buzzard is earned from the strange resemblance which a Carrion Vulture bears to a turkey, as it walks slowly and with a dignified air, stretching its long bare neck, and exhibiting the fleshy appendages which bear some likeness to the wattles of the turkey. This bird is chiefly found in North America.

GRIFFIN VULTURE.—*Gyps fulvus*.

THE COMMON, or GRIFFIN VULTURE, lives in many parts of the old world. In some places, where animals are allowed to lie unburied, or offal is thrown about in the streets, the Vulture is a very useful bird, eating the meat before it can decay. The colour of this Vulture is a yellowish-brown over the greater part of the body. The quill feathers of the tail and wings are nearly black, the ruff round the base of the neck is composed of long, white slender feathers, and the head and neck are clothed with short white down.

EGYPTIAN VULTURE.—*Néophron percnópterus.*

The Alpine, or Egyptian Vulture, lives in North Africa and Southern Europe. Sometimes it is called the White Crow, or Pharoah's Chicken. It eats rats, mice, lizards, and other animals. The general colour of the adult bird is nearly white, with the exception of the quill feathers of the wing, which are dark brown. The face, bill, and legs are bright yellow, so that the aspect of the bird is sufficiently curious. The sexes are clothed alike when adult.

GOLDEN EAGLE.—*A'quila chrysäétus.*

The Golden Eagle lives in many parts of the world. It is famous for its strength, swiftness, and courage. It mostly feeds on hares, rabbits, and other small animals, but often steals lambs out of the fold. Owing to the expanse of the wings and the power of the muscles, the flight of this bird is peculiarly bold and graceful. It sweeps through the air in a succession of spiral curves, rising with every spire, and making no perceptible motion with its wings.

BOLD EAGLE.—*Aquila audax.*

The Bold Eagle lives in Australia, and feeds on kangaroos, bustards, and other animals and birds. Since Sheep have been bred in Australia, it attacks and carries away the lambs. The colour of the Bold Eagle is a blackish-brown, becoming paler on the edges of the wings. The back of the neck takes a decided reddish hue. When young, the edge of each feather is tinged with red, and the tail barred.

LAUGHING FALCON.—*Herpetótheres cachinnans.*

The Laughing Falcon lives in Southern America, and derives its name from its curious cry, it sounds like a shrill laugh. It feeds on reptiles and fishes which it catches in lakes and rivers. The colour of this bird is nearly white, with a broad band of brown that passes over the back, wings, and the space round the eyes, and is prolonged into a belt that surrounds the neck, so that the bird looks as if it had been wrapped in a brown mantle fastened under the throat.

CRESTED, OR HARPY EAGLE.—*Thrasètus Harpyia.*

The beautiful Crested, or Harpy Eagle, lives in South America, and when angry, it ruffles up the fine grey and black crest on the top of its head. It is found in the forests. The general colour is blackish slate, the head is grey, and the chest and abdomen white, with a band of a darker hue across the chest. The tops of the feathers which compose the crest are black, and the tail is barred with black and grey. The beak and claws are black.

OSPREY.—*Pandion haliaëtus.*

The Osprey, or Fishing Hawk was once common in England, but is now seldom seen in the British Islands. It lives on fish, which it catches by dashing down into the sea or river at any fish which comes near the surface, and seizing it in its long curved claws. The general colour of the Osprey is dark brown, but it is variegated with black, grey, and white. The crown of the head and the nape of the neck are covered with long, grey-white feathers, streaked with dark brown. The under surface of the body is white, with the exception of a light brown band across the chest.

CINEREOUS, WHITE-TAILED, OR SEA-EAGLE.—*Haliaëtus albicilla.*

The Sea Eagle is still found in England, though it is very rarely seen. It generally lives on the sea coast, and catches fish nearly as well as the Osprey. It also eats hares, lambs, young fawns, and other animals. When full grown the tail is white. On the shores, the Sea Eagle seems to have regular hunting-grounds, and to make its rounds with perfect regularity, appearing at a certain spot at the same hour daily, keeping an anxious eye on the multitude of sea-fowl as they hover about the rock ledges in attendance upon their mates and families.

BALD, OR WHITE-HEADED EAGLE.—*Haliáëtus Leucocéphalus*.

The White-headed Eagle, or Bald Eagle, lives in America. It is strong and fierce, and eats large birds and many quadrupeds, besides being very fond of fish, which it often steals from the poor Osprey, just as it is going home with a fine fish for its children. Sometimes it feeds on dead animals, like the Vulture. The name of Bald, or White-headed Eagle, has been applied to this bird on account of the snowy-white colour of the head and neck, a peculiarity which renders it a most conspicuous bird. The remainder of the body is a deep chocolate brown, inclining to black along the back.

SOUTHERN CARACARA.—*Milvago Australis*.

The Southern Caracara lives in America, and feeds almost entirely on carrion. It is an impudent bird, as may be seen by Mr. Darwin's account. "They actually made an attack on a dog that was lying asleep close to one of the party, and the sportsmen had difficulty in preventing the wounded deer from being seized before their eyes. It is said that several together wait at the mouth of a rabbit-hole, and seize on the animal as it comes out. They were constantly flying on board the vessel when in the harbour, and it was necessary to keep a good look-out to prevent the leather from being torn from the rigging, and the meat and game from the stern. These birds are very mischevious, and most acquisitive; they will pick up almost anything from the ground; a large sized glazed hat was carried nearly a mile, as was a pair of heavy balls (bolas) used in catching cattle. Mr. Wilson experienced during the summer a more severe loss in their stealing a small Kater's compass in a red morocco case, which was never recovered. These birds, are, moreover, quarrelsome, and very passionate, tearing up the grass with their bills in rage. They build on the rocky cliffs of the sea-coast, but only in the small islets, and not in the two main lands." It is not quite so large as some of its brethren, but is quite as useful a bird. Its length is about eighteen inches, and its colour a greyish-brown upon the back and upper surface, and paler beneath, with reddish bands. The thighs are of a banded rusty-red, and the tail is yellowish-grey.

THE BRAZILIAN KITE or CARRANCHA lives in Southern America, where it is found to be a very useful, though not a very pleasant bird. It is a carrion eater, following the line of road in order to feed on the poor worn-out animals that sink tired out on the journey, and are left to perish by their hard-hearted drivers. It will watch the course pursued by hunters, and in hopes of obtaining the rejected portions of the slain animals, will follow them in their expeditions with as much perseverance and confidence as is exhibited by the American wolf. It also frequents the slaughter-houses, and is of great service in devouring the offal, which would otherwise be left to taint the air with its deadly odour. The name of Carrancha has been given to the bird on account of its rough cry, which is thought to resemble the word "carrancha." While uttering this cry, it bends its head very far back so that the top of the head almost touches the shoulders. It also eats little birds and quadrupeds.

BRAZILIAN KITE.
Polyborus Braziliensis.

The Brazilian Kite is blackish-brown, deepening to dull black from the top of the head, and varied across the neck and shoulders with wavy bands of dark brown on a greyish white, traversed by many narrow wavy bands of dusky brown. The bill is tinged with blue at the base, the claws are black, and the legs yellow. The keen sense of the bird will enable it to distinguish a feeble animal, or a dead carcass, at a wonderful distance, and its insatiable appetite is never appeased as long as there is a particle of flesh remaining on the bones.

BUZZARD.—*Búteo vulgáris.*

The Buzzard is a British bird, though seldom seen. It feeds on hares, rabbits, and other small quadrupeds. A Buzzard that was tamed by Mr. Thompson was a very amusing bird. It was fond of catching mice in a barn, darting at them as they ran over the floor, and striking at them through the straw. In many instances, the bird missed its stroke, but was always ready to make a fresh attack. It would also catch and kill rats, but preferred mice, probably because they gave it less trouble. It detested strangers, and used to fly fiercely at them and knock their hats over their ears, or fairly off their heads. A rather remarkable amusement in which this bird indulged, was to jump on its master's feet and untie his shoestrings. It would eat magpies and jackdaws, but did not seem to care very much for them. On one occasion a jackdaw had been shot, and fell into a mill dam. The Buzzard pounced on the dying bird, and grasping it in his talons, held it beneath the water until it was dead. Whether the act was intentional or not is not certain, but as the bird remained in so awkward a position with its legs wholly sunk in the water until the jackdaw was quite dead, the act does not seem to have been without some motive. The same bird was very fond of worms and grubs, and used to attend upon the potato-diggers, for the purpose of eating the worms and grubs that were thrown up. The flight of the Buzzard is rather variable. At times the bird seems inspired with the very soul of laziness, and contents itself with pouncing leisurely upon its prey. Sometimes, however, it rises high in the air, and displays a great power of wing and an easy grace of flight.

The handsome KITE still inhabits England, and may be known by its beautifully easy flight and its long forked tail. It is a destructive bird, feeding on game of all kinds; and often seizing chickens and ducklings out of the farm-yard. It also eats rats, mice, snakes, frogs, lizards, and is a great robber of other birds' nests, snatching the poor little things out of their warm nest before they are able to fly. When flying, it hardly seems to move its wings, but sails round in circles, and at last rises to such a height that it is hardly larger than a speck against the sky.

It is a good fisher, and is able to catch the fish by sweeping suddenly down upon them and snatching them up as they come to the surface. On account of its beautiful gliding flight, it is sometimes called the GLED, or GLEDE.

The Kite is possessed of a very docile and agreeable temper, and is easily tamed. Mr. Thompson records an instance, where a pair of these birds were taken from a nest near Loch Awe, in Argyleshire, and were so thoroughly domesticated that

KITE.—*Milvus regális.*

they were permitted to fly at liberty every morning. When thrown into the air, they always soared aloft in their graceful circling flights, displaying their wonderful command of wing and exulting in its exercise, but still so affectionate in their nature that they always returned to the hand of their owner when called. They were generally fed on rats and mice, and were very fond of catching the former animals as they were let loose from a cage. The bird has even been trained for purposes of falconry, and found to perform its task to the satisfaction of its owner.

SWALLOW-TAILED FALCON.

Elanoides furcátus.

THE SWALLOW-TAILED FALCON bears so strong a resemblance to the swallow, that it might easily be taken for a common swallow, or swift, as it flies circling in the air in search of the insect prey on which it feeds. Even the flight is very much of the same character in both birds, and the mode of feeding very similar. The usual food of the Swallow-tailed Kite consists of the larger insects, which it either catches on the wing, or snatches from the leaves as it shoots past the bushes. Various locusts, cicadæ, and other insects, are captured in this manner. It is very fond of wasps and their grubs, and has been noticed to excavate a wasp's nest, and to tear away the comb with its strong claws. Reptiles, such as small snakes, lizards, and frogs, also form part of the food of this elegant bird. While it is engaged in the pursuit of such prey, or in catching the large insects upon the branches, it may be approached and shot without much difficulty, as it is so intent upon its prey that it fails to notice its human foe.

Audubon found that when he had succeeded in killing one of these birds, he could shoot as many more as he chose, because they have a habit of circling round the body of their slaughtered comrade, and sweeping round it as if they were endeavouring to carry it away.

The nest of the Swallow-tailed Hawk is generally found on the very summit of some lofty rock or pine, and is almost always in the near vicinity of water. It is composed of small sticks externally, and is lined with grasses, moss, and feathers.

JERFALCON.—*Falco Gyrfalco.*

The Jerfalcon is another of our British birds. It was formerly much employed in the sport of hawking, and the young were procured from their nests by bold persons who would risk their lives upon the lofty cliffs of Iceland and Norway, on which its nest is made. The training of this Falcon is a difficult task, and is seldom finished in less than two months.

When at liberty in its native land, it seems to prefer birds to any other kind of prey, and will resolutely attack birds of considerable size, such as the heron or stork. It will also chase hares and rabbits, and in the pursuit of this swift game is so eager, that after knocking over one hare it will leave the maimed animal struggling on the ground while it goes off in chase of another. Although its home is in the chilly wastes of these northern regions, the bird is in no want of food, finding ample supply in the sea birds that swarm around the tall cliffs that jut into the waves, and being able from its great powers of flight to range over a vast extent of country in search of its daily food.

PEREGRINE FALCON.—*Falco peregrinus.*

The fine PEREGRINE FALCON is the bird which was usually employed in hawking, as it is bold, strong, swift, easily taught, and of an affectionate nature.

It was chiefly used to chase the Heron, and it is a fine sight to see these two noble birds attempting to rise above each other. The Falcon cannot strike unless it is above the prey, and the Heron tries to prevent it from doing so. Sometimes the Falcon shoots down upon the Heron's long sharp bill, and kills itself with the violence of the assault. It will chase many birds, especially curlews, grouse, and various kinds of game. When attacked by the Peregrine, the curlew and other water birds, always make for the sea, a sheet of water, or a river, because the Falcon does not like to risk itself by sweeping upon a floating object. The woodcock is often chased and killed by the Peregrine. The nest of the Peregrine is made upon lofty rocks.

The dash and fury with which this hawk makes its stoop is almost incredible. In a little coast town in Yorkshire, a part of a green-house had been divided off by wire so as to form an aviary, the roof of the aviary being the glass tiling of the greenhouse. In this edifice were placed a number of small birds, which attracted the attention of a Peregrine Falcon that was passing overhead. Totally unmindful of all obstacles, he shot crashing through the glass without injuring himself in the least, seized one of the terrified inmates, and carried it off in safety. Several other birds were found dead, apparently from fright.

The little MERLIN is another British hawk, and is employed for chasing the smaller birds of prey.

This beautiful little bird is almost invaluable to the young falconer, as it is so docile in disposition and so remarkably intelligent in character, that it repays his instructions much sooner than any of the more showy, but less teachable Falcons. Every movement of this admirable little hawk is full of life and vivacity; its head turns sharply from side to side as it sits on its master's hand, its eyes almost flame with fiery eagerness, and it ever and anon gives vent to its impatience by a volley of ear-piercing shrieks. There is, however, a singular capriciousness in the character of the Merlin, for it seems to be so sensitive to certain influences which are quite imperceptible to human beings, that the same individual which on one day or at one hour is full of fierce energy, chasing large and powerful birds of its own accord, following the course of the snipe with a wing as agile and far more enduring than its own, or shooting suddenly through the tangled branches of the underwood in pursuit of some prey that is fleeing to the leafy abode for refuge, will at another time become listless and even if it be induced to fly at its quarry, will turn suddenly away as if alarmed, and return languidly to its perch.

MERLIN.—*Hypotriorchis æsalon.*

With all these drawbacks, however, the Merlin is one of the very best little hawks that ever was put into training, for it can be taught to fly at anything that is indicated, and seems to care nothing for size.

KESTREL.—*Tinnúnculus Alaudárius.*

The common KESTREL is one of the most familiar of the British Hawks, being seen in almost every part of the country where a mouse, a lizard, or a beetle may be found. It may be easily distinguished while on the wing from any other hawk, by the peculiar manner in which it remains poised in air in a single spot, its head invariably pointing towards the wind, its tail spread, and its wings widely extended, almost as if it were a toy kite raised in the air by artificial means, and preserved in the same spot by a string. While hanging thus suspended in the air, its head is bent downwards, and its keen eyes glance restlessly in every direction, watching every blade of grass beneath its ken, and shooting down with unerring certainty of aim upon any unhappy fieldmouse that may be foolish enough to poke his red face out of his hole while the Kestrel is on the watch. The powers of the Kestrel's eye may be easily imagined by any one who has any experience of the field-mouse and the extreme difficulty of seeing the little creature while it is creeping among the grass straws. Its ruddy coat blends so well with the mould, and the grass blades bend so slightly under the pressure of its soft fur, that an unpractised eye would fail to detect the mouse even if its precise locality were pointed out.

The number of field-mice consumed by this hawk is very great, for it is hardly possible to open the stomach of a Kestrel without finding the remains of one or more of these destructive little animals. On account of its mouse-loving propensities, the Kestrel is a most useful bird to the farmer.

THE GOSHAWK is a large and magnificent bird; sometimes, but not very often, seen in England. It is good at the chase, but better adapted to pursue quadrupeds than birds; and in the chase of hares and rabbits is not to be equalled. Its hunting is singularly like that of the chetah, which has already been mentioned in the volume on the Mammalia. Like that animal, it is not nearly so swift as its prey, and therefore is obliged to steal upon them, and seize its victim by a sudden and unexpected pounce. When it has once grasped its prey it is rarely found to loose its hold, even by the most violent struggles or the most furious attack. The gripe is so enormously powerful, that a Goshawk has often been observed to pounce upon a large hare, and to maintain its hold even though the animal sprang high into the air, and then rolled upon the ground in the vain hope of shaking off his feathered antagonist. Only the female bird is able to cope with so powerful a creature as a full-grown hare or rabbit, for the male, although more swift of wing, and therefore

GOSHAWK.—*Astur palumbárius.*

better adapted for chasing birds than the female, is comparatively feeble. When it has once seized its prey, it is full of exultation, and being generally rather of a ferocious disposition, is apt to turn savagely upon the hand that attempts to remove it from its victim. Its temper, indeed, is so bad, that if it should happen to escape from its bonds and get among other Falcons it will almost certainly attack and kill as many of them as it can reach. For the same reason it needs to be kept constantly hooded, and is less to be trusted at liberty than any other Falcon.

SPARROW HAWK.—*Accipiter Nisus.*

The Sparrow Hawk is a well known English bird, though like other beasts and birds of prey, it becomes more scarce as land is more cultivated.

Although the Sparrow Hawk inhabits England in great numbers, it is not so often seen as might be imagined, for it is a most wild, shy, and wary bird, and never ventures near human dwellings, or within a considerable distance of human beings, unless urged by hunger or carried away by the ardour of pursuit. As a general rule, to get within gunshot of a Sparrow Hawk is no easy matter; but if the Hawk be watched as he is hovering about a flock of sparrows or other small birds, he may be approached without much difficulty, his entire attention being engaged on his expected prey. Indeed, while engaged in the chase, the ardour of this bird is so great, that all its faculties seem to be absorbed in the ruling passion, and it is evidently unmindful of anything but its flying prey. A Sparrow Hawk has been known to dash furiously at a man who endeavoured to rescue a small bird which it had attacked. The courage of the Sparrow Hawk is of the most reckless character, for the bird will fly unhesitatingly at almost any other inhabitant of air, no matter what its size may be. In consequence of the headlong courage possessed by this handsome little Hawk, it is very valuable to the falconer if properly trained, for it will dash at any quarry which may be pointed out to it. Unfortunately, however, the Sparrow Hawk is one of the most difficult and refractory of pupils, slow at receiving a lesson and quick at forgetting it.

The Secretary Bird is a most useful creature in Southern Africa, where it is found in numbers. It feeds almost entirely upon reptiles, and especially upon snakes, which it destroys and devours; heedless of their venomed fangs. When it meets with a snake, it strikes violently with its wings, and occasionally pecks sharply with its strong beak.

It will then rise in the air, fly away for a few yards, and again return to the attack, continuing this mode of action, until it has killed the snake; which is then devoured. It will sometimes pick up the snake in its bill, soar to a great height, and then let the serpent drop on a hard rock, so as to kill it without trouble. It also feeds much on frogs and toads.

It is called the Secretary bird, because the long feathers on its head, look like pens stuck behind the ears.

The nest of the Secretary is built on the summit of a lofty tree, and contains two or three large white eggs.

SECRETARY BIRD.—*Serpentárius Secretárius.*

HEN HARRIER.—*Circus cyáneus.*

THE HEN HARRIER lives in England, and may be readily distinguished from the other hawks by the manner in which the feathers radiate around the eyes, forming a kind of funnel-shaped depression, somewhat similar to, but not so perfect as that of the owl. This structure is thought to be serviceable to the bird, in giving it a wide range of vision in its hunting excursions. The flight of the Harrier is very low, seldom being more than a few yards above the ground, and as the bird flies along it beats every bush, and pries into every little covert in search of prey. There are few of the smaller animals that do not fall victims to the Hen Harrier, which is always ready to pick up a field-mouse, a lizard, a small snake, a newt, or a bird, and will even pounce upon so large a bird as a partridge or pheasant. Sometimes it sits on a stone or small hillock, and from that post keeps up a careful watch on the surrounding country, sweeping off as soon as it observes indications of any creature on which it may feed.

The flight of the Hen Harrier, although it is not remarkable for its power, is yet very swift, easy, and gliding, and as the bird quarters the ground after its prey, is remarkably graceful.

Like the Kestrel, the Hen Harrier appears to have regular hunting-grounds, and is very punctual in its visits. The nest of this bird is generally placed under the shadow of some convenient furze-bush, and is composed of a few sticks thrown loosely together, in which are deposited four or five very pale blué eggs.

JARDINES HARRIER is a native of Australia, and is very remarkable on account of the singular manner in which the plumage is covered with circular spots of pure white on a dark chestnut ground.

There is a good account of this bird in Mr. Gould's beautiful work on the Birds of Australia.

According to Gould, it is generally found in plains, and specially frequents the wide and luxuriant grass flats that intervene between the mountain ranges.

Like all the birds of the same genus, it is never seen to soar, but sweeps over the surface of the ground at a low elevation, seeking after the mice, reptiles, small birds, and other creatures on which it feeds. It is very fond of small snakes and frogs, and in order to obtain them may be seen hovering over the marshes, or beating the wet ground after the fashion of the hen harrier.

It is seldom known to perch on trees, preferring to take its stand on some large stone or elevated hillock from which it can survey the surrounding land. The nest of this bird is supposed to be built on the ground, over-shadowed by some bush or tuft of grass, like that of other harriers, and placed upon the top of one of the numerous "scrub" hills.

JARDINES HARRIER.—*Circus Jardinii.*

CANADA OWL.—*Súrnia úlula.*

The Owls are easily known by their big round heads, the manner in which the large eyes are set in front of the face, and the curious circle of stiff feathers which surround the eyes.

They are almost entirely birds of night, pursuing their prey during the hours of darkness, and being so greatly incommoded by daylight that they are partly blinded by the glare and cannot direct their flight.

The Canada or Hawk Owl lives in North America, Northern Asia, and Europe. It is very common in Canada.

The food of the Canada Owl consists chiefly of rats, mice, and insects, during the summer months; but in the winter, while rats and mice keep within their homes, and the insects are as yet in their pupa state, the Canada Owl turns its attention to birds, and will even chase and kill so powerful a bird as the ptarmigan. It is a very bold bird, and has been known to pounce upon and carry away wounded game that has fallen before the sportsman's gun. While chasing the ptarmigan it follows the course of their migration, hanging about the flocks and making sad havock in their numbers.

Although so bold and so successful a hunter, the Hawk Owl is by no means a large bird, being only from fifteen to seventeen inches in length, and therefore not equalling the common hen harrier in dimensions. Its nest is generally made on the top of a tree, and not in the hollow of the trunk as is commonly the case with the Owls, which usually take possession of a hollow in some dead branch and lay their eggs on the soft decaying wood, or make their home in a convenient crevice of some old building. The male Hawk Owl is rather less than the female, as is the case with most predaceous birds.

The plumage is closer than that of the generality of Owls, whose feathers are fringed with delicate downy filaments, for the purpose of enabling them to float noiselessly through the air, for the Hawk Owl is a swift-winged bird, and obtains its prey by fair chase.

SNOWY OWL.—*Nyctea nivea.*

The Great Snowy Owl is found in the northern regions of the world, and has occasionally made its appearance in England. It is a very large bird, with great shining eyes, and has often frightened persons who have come upon it suddenly at night. It eats rats, mice, and other creatures, and is very useful in catching and devouring the lemmings which pass over vast tracts of country, devastating them like clouds of locusts. On this account, the Snowy Owl is an useful bird. Sometimes it eats fish, and catches them by sitting on some stump projecting over the water, and hooking out the fish with one foot, while it clings to its perch with the other.

The colour of an old Snowy Owl is pure white without any markings whatever; but in the earlier years of its life, its plumage is covered with numerous dark-brown spots and bars, caused by a dark tip to each feather. Upon the breast and abdomen, these markings form short abrupt curves, but on the back and upper surface they are nearly straight. The beak and claws are black. The length of the male Snowy Owl is about twenty-two inches, and that of the female twenty-six or twenty-seven.

COQUIMBO, OR BURROWING OWL.—*Athéne cunicutria.*

THE odd little BURROWING OWL, with its long legs and wise looking head, inhabits many parts of America, and is remarkable not only for its habit of burrowing in the ground, but from the sociable manner in which it lives in company with the curious marmot called the prairie dog. Sometimes a rattlesnake is found in the burrow, but the reptile is only an intruder, come to pick up a young Owl or a little marmot. Generally the Owl takes advantage of the burrows made and deserted by the marmot, but in some places it is obliged to work for itself, and does so in rather a clumsy fashion.

Lizards and other reptiles have also been found in the burrows of the prairie dog. While sitting on the little earth mounds, or moving among the burrows, the Coquimbo Owl presents a very curious likeness to the prairie dog itself, and at a little distance might easily be taken for the little marmot as it sits erect at the mouth of its domicile.

The colour of the Burrowing Owl is a rather rich brown, upon the upper parts of the body, diversified with a number of small grey-white spots, and altogether darker upon the upper surface of the wings. The under parts are greyish-white. The length of the bird is not quite eleven inches. The cry of this curious bird is unlike that of any other Owl, and bears a strong resemblance to the short, sharp bark of the prairie dog.

Another curious little Owl is sometimes found in England, and has therefore gained a place among the British birds. This is Tengmalm's Owl, or Death Bird, the latter name having been given to it on account of a common superstition that reigns among several of the North-American Indian tribes. When an Indian hears one of these birds uttering its melancholy cry, he whistles towards the spot from whence the sound proceeded, and if the bird does not answer him, he looks for a speedy death.

This species is at first sight not unlike the Little Owl, but may be at once distinguished from that bird by the structure of its legs and toes, and the thick feathery coating with which they are clad. It is a very common bird over the whole of the inhabited portions of North America, but is frequently found in Norway, Sweden, Russia, and even in Northern France and Italy. It is a nocturnal bird, seldom wandering from its home during the hours of daylight, as it is almost blinded by the unaccustomed glare, and may be easily captured by the hand while thus bewildered. The nest of the Tengmalm's Owl is generally made of grass, and is placed about half-way up some convenient pine-tree. The eggs are seldom more than two in number, are pure white in colour, and not quite so globular as is the case with the generality of owls' eggs.

TENGMALM'S OWL.

Nyctale funérea.

The colour of this bird is more rich and better defined than that of the Little Owl. The whole of the upper parts of the body are a rich chocolate-brown, dotted and splashed with many white markings, which are very minute upon the top of the head, and larger upon the back and wings, some indeed being arranged on the lower portions of the wings so as to form irregular stripes. Similar white spots are placed on the tail, which is usually of a dark brown. The eye disk is greyish-white, excepting a bold black-brown ring just round the eye. The under portions of the body are greyish-white, covered with numerous brown bars and spots, and the plumage of the legs and toes is also grey-white sprinkled with brown spots. The size of the Tengmalm's Owl is nearly the same as that of the Little Owl.

VIRGINIAN EARED OWL.

Bubo Virginiánus.

The Virginian Eared Owl is a well known inhabitant of many parts of America. It is a very large bird, nearly equalling the great Owl in magnitude, and being in no way inferior in strength or courage. This species in former days did great damage among the poultry of the agriculturists, being a bold as well as a voracious bird. Now, however, the ever-ready rifle of the farmer has thinned its numbers greatly, and has inspired the survivors with such awe, that they mostly keep clear of cultivated lands, and confine themselves to seeking after their legitimate prey.

The Virginian Eared or Horned Owl is a terrible destroyer of game, snatching up grouse, partridges, hares, ducks, sparrows, squirrels, and many other furred and feathered creatures, and not unfrequently striving after larger quarry. The wild turkey is a favourite article of diet with this Owl; but on account of the extreme wariness of the turkey nature, the depredator finds an unseen approach to be no easy matter. The usual mode in which the Owl catches the turkey is, to find out a spot where its intended prey is quietly sleeping at night, and then to swoop down suddenly upon the slumbering bird before it awakes. Sometimes, however, the Owl is baffled in a very curious manner. When the turkey happens to be roused by the rush of the winged foe, it instinctively ducks its head and spreads its tail flatly over its back. The Owl striking upon the slippery plain of stiff tail feathers, finds no hold for its claws, and glides off the back of its intended victim, which immediately dives into the brushwood before the Owl can recover from the surprise of its unexpected failure.

The nest of this bird is extremely large, and consists of a large bundle of sticks, grass, leaves, and feathers, placed in the fork of some large bough, and containing three or four white eggs. The colour of the Virginian Eared Owl is reddish brown upon the upper surface, mottled with various splashes of black.

LONG-EARED OWL.—*Otus vulgaris.*

The Long-eared Owl lives in England, and is an odd looking bird, on account of the feathery tuft that stands up on the top of its head. It flies by night, and eats mice and young birds which it has been seen to take from the nest. It is easily tamed, as may be seen by this account of a young Long-eared Owl called Blinker, which was put into the same closet with a cat named Fanny, and her kittens.

"Pussy regarded him at first with very suspicious looks; but the poor bird, feeling pleased with the dim light and pussy's soft warm coat, soon nestled up to her. This act of confidence on Blinker's part appeared to affect Fanny favourably, and she at once purred him a welcome. From this time they were fast friends, and many mice did she good-naturedly provide Blinker with in common with her own kitten. When he grew large enough, he used to sit on the side of her basket, and would never settle quietly for the night until the two cats were asleep in their bed.

"It was quite beautiful to observe the warm affection which grew up between the Owlet and the kitten. The only cause of discord that we ever noticed between the two, was when the kitten would play with a living mouse. This evidently hurt Blinker's feelings, for he would always pounce down and seize the mouse by the back of its neck, and kill it in a moment. Still, he had a sense of justice in his nature; for when the mouse was dead, he would drop it down to its rightful owner.

"I had him for a year, and was much attached to him; but he fell ill, and went the way of all pets."

WHITE, OR BARN OWL.—*Strix flammea.*

The Barn Owl is very common in England, residing in barns, hollow trees, or ruined buildings, often in company with jackdaws and starlings. It feeds almost entirely on mice, though it will sometimes eat little birds, and one Owl is more useful to the farmer than a hundred rat or mouse-traps, for it catches and eats the field-mice which will not come into houses, and cannot easily be decoyed into traps.

In feeding its young families, of which it has two in each year, it consumes a vast number of these tiresome little animals.

In the evening dusk, when the mice begin to stir abroad in search of a mole, the Owl starts in search of the mice, and with noiseless flight quarters the ground in a sportsmanlike and very regular manner, watching with its great round eyes every movement of a grass-blade, and catching with its sensitive ears every sound that issues from behind. Not a field-mouse can come within ken of the bird's eye, or make the least rustling among the leaves within hearing of the Owl's ear, that is not detected and captured. The claws are the instruments by which the Owl seizes its victim, and it does not employ the beak until it desires to devour the prey.

Sometimes the Owl has been detected in robbing the pigeons' nests of their young; but such conduct seems to be very rare, as there are many instances on record where the Owl has actually inhabited the same cote with the pigeons without touching their young or disturbing the peace of the parents. This Owl is also an experienced fisher, and has been seen to drop quietly upon the water and return to its nest bearing in its claws a perch which it had captured.

TRINIDAD GOAT-SUCKER.—*Steatornis Caripensis.*

The Goat-suckers or Nightjars are also night-flying birds, but they feed upon insects instead of mice. They all have soft plumage, great large round eyes, and very large mouths, so as to catch the insects as they fly through the air.

One of the most curious of these birds is the Guacharo, which lives in certain vast caverns in Trinidad. The natives catch it when young by going into the caverns and knocking the birds off their nests with long poles. It is a valuable bird, as when taken young, it is one lump of fat, which is melted down in clay pots, and produces a very soft and limpid oil, which does not easily become rancid.

The colour of this curious bird is a ruddy fawn, mottled with dark brown, and spotted here and there with square white marks, the squares being mostly set with one of the angles upwards, in lozenge fashion.

EUROPEAN GOAT-SUCKER.—*Caprimulgus Europæus*.

The common Nightjar, Goat-sucker, or Fern Owl, lives in England, and is very plentiful in some places, provided that they be at some distance from towns. In the New Forest the Nightjars abound, and may be heard every evening as they fly round the trees in chase of the insects, or sit upon the branches, uttering their curious whirring cry. It is a very useful bird, because it feeds much on the cockchaffers, which are among the most destructive of the insect tribe, and unless their numbers were checked by birds and other means, would be more terrible than the locusts of the east.

The Nightjar also feeds on moths of various kinds, and catches them by sweeping quickly and silently among the branches of the trees near which the moth tribes most love to congregate. While engaged in their sport, they will occasionally settle on a bank, a wall, a post, or other convenient perch, crouch downward until they bring their head almost on a level with their feet, and utter the peculiar churning note which has earned for them the name of Churn-Owls, Jar-Owls, and Spinners. Their cry has been rather well compared to that sound which is produced by the larger beetles of the night, but of course much louder, and with the addition of the characteristic "chur-r-r!—chur-r-r!" Sometimes, although but seldom, the Nightjar utters its cry while on wing. When it settles, it always seats itself along a branch, and almost invariably with its head pointing towards the trunk of the tree.

Athough rather a shy bird, and avoiding the presence of mankind, it is bold enough on occasion, and when it finds an abundance of food, or when it desires to defend its young, it cares little for any strange form, whether of man or beast.

LONG-TAILED GOAT-SUCKER.—*Scotornis climacúrus.*

The Long-Tailed Goat-sucker lives in Western Africa, and is remarkable for the length of its tail and the general outline of the body, which looks something like that of a Cuckoo. It is really not a large bird, but its long wings and tail and its soft, thick plumage, make it appear larger than really is the case.

The name of Goat-sucker was applied to these birds from a silly notion, still believed in some places, that they were in the habit of coming by night and sucking the milk from the goats as they lay asleep.

In the colour of its plumage it is rather a handsomer bird than the generality of Goat-suckers, owing to the quantity of white which is laid in bold markings on several parts of its feathers. The chin is white, as is also a streak that passes from the corner of the mouth. A broad band of white passes across the extremities of the lesser wing coverts, and there is a smaller band of cream colour upon the tips of the greater coverts. Another beautifully white band is drawn across the middle of the first six primary feathers, and the remaining primaries have a spot of white on their tips. The rest of the plumage is variegated with black and brown, warmed here and there with a more ruddy hue. The tail is also white in several parts, and has a number of very narrow dark bars across the middle pair of feathers.

LEONA GOAT-SUCKER.—*Macrodipteryx longipennis.*

The Leona Goat-sucker also comes from Western Africa, and is remarkable for the curious feathers which start from the wings, and trail far behind as the bird flies. For the greater part of their length they are nearly bare of web, having only a few scattered threads of feathery substance, but at the end they expand into two broad tips. These long feathers are only found in the full-grown male bird, and their use is not known.

The plumage of the Leona Nightjar is very prettily marked with spots and bars of rusty-red and black upon the usual brown ground. Every primary feather possesses nine rusty-red spots, and as many of a black hue, and there are many other spots and bars scattered over the body and wings. There is a considerable amount of creamy white upon the scapularies, a few white mottlings upon the throat of the male, and a reddish-white stripe down the outer web of the two exterior tail-feathers.

The Swallows perform the same task by day as the Goat-suckers by night, chasing and catching the insects as they fly through the air. They are smaller birds than the Goat-suckers, and therefore feed on smaller insects, gnats and such like creatures being their usual prey. In all these birds the beak is very short, very wide, the mouth is enormously large, and the wings are long, sharp, and pointed, so as to cut through the air with the greatest speed. Their tails are more or less forked, and their speed while on the wing is very great.

The NEEDLE-TAILED SWALLOW comes from Australia, and derives its name from the tips of the tail feathers, which project in sharp short points, like a number of needles. Mr. Gould writes of this bird:—

"So exclusively is this bird a tenant of the air, that I never in any instance saw it perch, and but rarely sufficiently near the earth to admit of a successful shot; it is only late in the evening and during lowery weather that such an object can be accomplished. With the exception of the crane, it is certainly the most lofty as well as the most vigorous flier of the

AUSTRALIAN NEEDLE-TAILED SWALLOW.

Acánthylis caudacuta.

Australian birds. I have frequently observed in the middle of the hottest days, while lying prostrate on the ground with my eyes directed upwards, the cloudless blue sky peopled at an immense elevation by hundreds of these birds, performing extensive curves and sweeping flights, doubtless attracted thither by the insects that soar aloft during serene weather."

SWIFT.—*Cpýsclus apus.*

THE COMMON SWIFT is very well known in England, as it loves to build its nest in the eaves of houses, and is very fond of thatched roofs, burrowing a hole well into the thatch, and making the nest at the end of the tunnel. When flying, the Swift screams continually, and is sometimes called the Jacky-screamer in consequence.

When they have become accustomed to human beings, they are wonderfully indifferent to their presence, and will permit their movements to be watched without displaying any signs of fear. I well remember a certain street which was much favoured by the Swifts, who congregated in such great numbers, that they became a positive nuisance on account of the continual screaming which they kept up. The houses were mostly of a very ancient fashion, and their eaves were so low, that a man could introduce his hand into the Swifts' tunnels merely by standing on a chair. Yet the birds cared nothing for their apparent danger, even though their nests were several times robbed of their contents. At one time, the small boys, who abounded in the neighbourhood, took a fancy to manufacture bows and arrows, with which they kept up a persevering fire upon the Swifts, as they went to and fro upon their avocations, or visited and returned from their nests. The birds, however, looked upon these weapons with supreme contempt, and never troubled themselves in the least about them.

In general, the Swift loves to build its nest in a hole under a roof, whether slated, tiled or thatched, preferring, however, the warm, thick straw-thatch to the tile or slate. Sometimes it makes a hole in the thatch, through which it gains access to the nest, but in most instances it makes use of some already existing crevice for that purpose.

THE ESCULENT SWALLOW is found in Java, and is a valuable and remarkable bird, as it produces the celebrated "birds' nests" of which the Chinese are so fond when made into soup.

These nests could hardly be recognised as specimens of bird architecture by any one who had not previously seen them, as they look much more like a set of sponges, corals, or fungi, than nests of birds. They are most irregular in shape, are fastened to each other, and are so rudely made, that the hollow in which the eggs and young are intended to live, is barely visible. They are always placed against the face of a steep rock, generally upon the side of one of the tremendous caverns in Java and other places where these strange birds love to dwell. The men who procure the nests are lowered by ropes from above, and their occupation is always considered as perilous in the extreme.

ESCULENT SWALLOW.
Collocália nidífica.

While adhering to the rocks, or when gathered into baskets, the nests are not at all attractive in their aspect, and it is not until they have been carefully washed and cleansed, that they begin to show their structure, shining through its partially transparent substance. The nests are of very different value, those which have been used in rearing a brood of young being comparatively low in price, while those which are quite new and nearly white, are held in uch esteem, that they are worth their weight in silver, When placed in water sand allowed to remain in soak, the nests, being made of a partially gelatinous substance, begin to soften and swell, and when thoroughly dressed, are said to bear some resemblance to rather stiff turtle fat. To European palates, however, they appear very insipid, and not worthy of the great value which is set upon them by the Chinese.

The precise material of these nests is not clearly known. It is certainly animal substance to some extent, although certain vegetable matters, such as the gelatinous fuci or sea-weeds, may be admixed with it. Whatever may be the basis of the nutriment that forms these nests, it is clear that a very large portion of it is furnished by certain glands which pour out a viscid secretion.

SWALLOW.—*Hirundo Rústica.*

The common Swallow is very familiar as an English bird, and is more attached to man and his habitations than almost any other species.

The nest of the Swallow is always placed in some locality where it is effectually sheltered from wind and rain. Generally it is constructed under the eaves of houses, but as it is frequently built within disused chimneys, it has given to the species the popular title of Chimney Swallow. The bird is probably attracted to the chimney by the warmth of some neighbour fire.

The nest is composed externally of mud or clay, which is brought by the bird in small lumps, and stuck in irregular rows so as to build up the sides of its little edifice. There is an attempt at smoothing the surface of the nest, but each lump of clay is easily distinguishable upon the spot where it has been stuck. While engaged at the commencement of its labours, the Swallow clings perpendicularly to the wall of the house or chimney, holding with its sharp little claws to any small projection, and supporting itself by the pressure of its tail against the wall. The interior of the nest is lined with grasses and other soft substances, and after it has been inhabited by a young brood, becomes very offensive to the nostrils and unpleasant to the touch, in consequence of the large ticks which are peculiar to the birds of this tribe, and which swarm in the nest.

There are sometimes two broods in the year, and when the second brood has been hatched at a very late period of the year, the young are frequently deserted and left to starve by their parents, who are unable to resist the innate impulse that urges them to seek a warmer climate. It has occasionally happened that the parents have remained for some time in order to bring up their young brood.

FAIRY MARTINS.—*Hirundo Ariel.*

The Fairy Martin lives in Australia, and is very remarkable for the curious nest which it builds.

The nest of the Fairy Martin has a very close resemblance to a common oil flask, and reminds the observer of the flask-shaped nests which are constructed by the pensile oriole and similar birds, although made of harder material. The Fairy Martin builds its curious house of mud and clay, which it kneads thoroughly in its beak before bringing it to the spot where it will be required. Six or seven birds work at each nest, one remaining in the interior enacting the part of chief architect, while others act as hodsmen, and bring material as fast as it is required. Except on wet days, this bird only works in the evening and early morning, as the heat of mid-day seems to dry the mud so rapidly that it cannot be rightly kneaded together. The mouths, or "spouts" of these nests vary from eight to ten inches in length, and point indifferently in all directions. The diameter of the widest portion of the nest is very variable, and ranges between four and seven inches.

The exterior of the nest is as rough as that of the common swallow of England, but the interior is comparatively smooth, and is lined with feathers and fine grass. The eggs are generally four or five in number, and the bird rears two broods in the course of the year.

HOUSE MARTINS.—*Chelidon urbica*.

RESEMBLING the common swallow in habits and general appearance, the HOUSE MARTIN may easily be distinguished from that bird by the large white patch upon the lower part of the back. In the dusk of evening the Martins may often be seen flying about at so late an hour, that their bodies are almost invisible in the dim and fading twilight, and their presence is only shown by the white patches upon their backs, which reflect every fading ray, and bear a singular resemblance to white moths or butterflies darting though the air.

This beautiful little bird is found in all parts of England, and is equally familiar with the swallow and sand Martin. It places its clay-built nest principally under the shelter afforded by human habitations, and becomes so trustful and fearless that it will often fix its nest close to a window, and will rear its young without being dismayed at the near presence of human beings.

It is rather a curious fact that the Martin should be so capricious in taste, as has frequently been observed. The birds will often take a great fancy to one side of a house, and will place whole rows of their nests under the eaves, totally neglecting the remaining sides of the house, even though they offer equal or superior accommodation. A north-eastern aspect is in great favour with the Martins, and I lately observed a very great number of their nests affixed to the eastern walls of a row of houses, together with several isolated cottages, and, on a careful examination, could not see a single nest upon any other part of the buildings.

The nest of this species is extremely variable in shape and size, no two being precisely similar in both respects. Generally the edifice is cup-shaped, with the rim closely pressed against the eaves of some friendly house, and having a small semicircular aperture cut out of the edge, in order to permit the ingress and egress of the birds. Sometimes, however, the nest is supported on a kind of solid pedestal, composed also of mud, and often containing nearly as much material as would have made an ordinary nest. These pedestals are generally constructed in spots where the Martin finds that her nest does not obtain sufficient support from the wall.

The Rollers are rather curious and very handsome birds, with beautiful feathers. They feed on insects, but do not fly as well as the Swallows and Goat-suckers.

Although tolerably common on several parts of the Continent, the GARRULOUS ROLLER is at the present time a very rare visitant to this country. There seems, however, to be reason to believe that in former days, when England was less cultivated and more covered with pathless woods, the Roller was frequently seen in the ancient forests, and that it probably built its nest in the hollows of trees, as it does in the German forests at the present day.

GARRULOUS ROLLER.

Corácias Gárrula.

Africa is the legitimate home of the Roller, which passes from that land in the early spring, and makes its way to Europe, *viâ* Malta and the Mediterranean Islands, which afford it resting-places during its long journey. Accordingly, in those islands the Rollers are found in great plenty, and, as they are considered a great delicacy when fat and in good condition, they are killed in considerable numbers, and exposed for sale like pigeons, whose flesh they are said to resemble. Even in its flight it possesses something of the pigeon character, having often been observed while flying at a considerable elevation to "tumble" after the manner of the well-known tumbler pigeons. It is rather curious that throughout Asia Minor, the Rollers and magpies were always found in close proximity to each other.

Mr. Thompson records a very curious anecdote of this bird, a specimen of which was seen flying across the grounds of the Duke of Leinster, in September, 1831, and was pursued by a large number of rooks, who were mobbing it after their usual custom whenever they meet with a strange bird. The Roller did not seem to be in the least disconcerted; but, instead of endeavouring to escape, darted repeatedly among its foes, as if for the purpose of increasing their irritation.

The general tint of the head, neck, breast, and abdomen is that peculiar green-blue termed "verditer" by artists, changing into pale green in certain lights, and deepening into deep rich azure upon the shoulders. The back is a warm chestnut.

BRAZILIAN MOTMOT.

Mómotus Braziliensis.

The Motmots are so called because their cry resembles the word "mot-mot" frequently repeated.

The Brazilian Motmot is a very solitary bird, being seldom seen except by those who care to penetrate into the deepest recesses of the tropical forests. In its habits, it is not at all unlike the common fly-catcher of England, delighting to sit motionless upon a branch that overlooks one of the open spaces that are found in all forests, or that commands a view of a path made by man or beast. On its perch it remains as still as if carved in wood, and sits apparently without thought or sensation until a tempting insect flies within easy reach. It then launches itself upon its prey, catches the insect in its bill, and returning to its perch, settles down again into its former state of languid tranquility. The Motmot is not formed for long or active flight, as its wings are short and rounded, and the plumage, especially about the head, very loosely set.

Some writers say that the Motmots do not confine themselves to such small prey as insects, but that they steal young birds out of their nests, and are also in the habit of eating eggs.

All the Motmots are about the size of the common magpie, and are remarkably handsome birds, their plumage being tinted with green, blue, scarlet, and other brilliant colours.

MASSENA'S TROGON.—*Trogon Massenæ.*

MEXICAN TROGON.—*Trogon Mexicánus.*

THE TROGONS are wonderfully beautiful birds, their plumage being of the brightest hues of green, azure, crimson, and gold. They differ greatly in their colouring according to their age.

These beautiful birds are found in the Old and New Worlds, those which inhabit the latter locality being easily distinguished by their deeply barred tails. Those of the Old World are generally found in Ceylon, Sumatra, Java, and Barneo, while only a single species, the Narina Trogon, is as yet known to inhabit Africa.

MASSENA'S TROGON lives in Central America, and is light golden green above, and scarlet below. The MEXICAN TROGON has something of the same colours, but has a very pretty collar of pure white round the neck.

CUBA TROGON.—*Priótelus temnurus.*

MALABAR TROGON.—*Harpactes Malabricus.*

The Cuba Trogon lives in the country from which it derives its name. It runs about the branches of trees and picks out the insects that try to hide under the bark. The tail of this bird looks as if the feathers had been trimmed with scissors.

According to Gould, it bears a singular resemblance to the woodpeckers, both in its habits and in the general formation of its plumage. Like those birds, it runs about the trunks and branches of trees, peers into the hollows, and dislodges from under the bark the insects on which it feeds.

The Malabar Trogon is found in Malabar, where it sits idly on a branch all day, and hardly stirs until night, when it becomes very lively, and catches insects as they traverse the branches.

BEAUTIFUL TROGON.—*Calúrus antisiánus*.

The Beautiful Trogon is a native of South America, and well deserves its name, as it is not only richly gorgeous in the colours of its plumage, but is also elegant in form. On account of the looseness of its feathers it is not able to chase insects in the air with as much ease as is exhibited by the firmer-feathered Trogons, and is found to make its diet chiefly upon berries, fruits, and the insects which it can pick off the branches without being forced to pursue them on the wing. While engaged in the search after food, it is an active bird, running about the boughs with great agility, and clinging with its feet in every attitude, head downward, like the parrots.

The whole upper parts of this bird are rich golden green, the under surface is carmine, and the wings are jetty black. Although so brilliant in colouring, it is not so easily seen as might be supposed, as its colour harmonizes well with the foliage and bark of the trees among which it dwells, and even the rich carmine of its under surface is not very conspicuous in that land of flowers.

WHITE-FACED BARBET.—*Mónasa leucops.*

The Barbets, or Puff Birds, clearly form a connecting link between the trogons and the kingfishers, possessing several of the peculiarities of the former birds, together with some characteristics of the latter.

In shape they bear a close resemblance to the kingfishers, and none of them are of any great size. Their food consists chiefly of insects, which they chase much after the manner of the woodpeckers, prying into the hollows of trees, and striking away the bark in their endeavours to secure the concealed prey. They can cling to the upright trunk of a tree, and support themselves by the pressure of their short stiff tails against the bark. They also possess some of the habits which belong to the flycatchers, and taking their perch upon a twig, will wait patiently until an unfortunate insect passes within a short distance, when they will launch themselves on the devoted creature, and return to the identical twig from which they started. The White-Faced Barbet lives in South America.

To all appearance the Barbets are dull birds, chained as it were to a single spot, and apparently feeling every movement a source of trouble. But to the Barbet itself, this kind of inactive life constitutes its best happiness; and we should be wrong to attribute sadness and melancholy to it. While sitting upon the twig which it has chosen for its perch, the Barbet has a curious habit of puffing out its plumage, so as to transform itself into an almost cylindrical ball of feathers.

LAUGHING JACKASS.—*Dacelo gigas.*

The odd looking bird called the Laughing Jackass, on account of its cry, is found in Australia, where it startles the stranger by its loud yelling laugh, which it utters by night. Though a kingfisher, it cares little about fish, feeding mostly on insects, mice, and reptiles.

At the rising and setting of the sun the Laughing Jackass becomes very lively, and is the first to welcome the approach of dawn, and to chant its strange exulting song at the return of darkness.

BUFF DACELO.—*Dacélo cervina.*

The Buff Dacelo inhabits the thickly wooded portions of the northern and north-western districts of Australia, where it may be seen and heard sitting on the topmost branches of the loftiest trees, taking observations of the surrounding country, and yelling in a most unmusical manner. When three or four pairs of these birds get together upon a single tree, they become quite excited by mutual noise, and make such a horrid uproar that nothing can be heard except their deafening outcries.

The Australian Kingfisher is a resident in New South Wales from August to December or January, and then passes to a warmer climate. Like the preceding birds, it cares little for the presence of water, making its subsistence chiefly on large insects, such as locusts caterpillars, grasshoppers, and cicadæ, which it seizes in its bill, and beats violently against the ground before eating them. It is also very fond of small crabs and other crustaceans. Mr. Gould mentions that the stomachs of Australian Kingfishers that had been shot were found crammed with these creatures. To obtain them it is in the habit of frequenting the sea-shore, and pouncing upon the crabs, shrimps, prawns, and various other creatures as they are thrown on the strand by the retiring tide, or forced to take refuge in shallow rock-pools, whence they can easily be extracted by the long bill of this voracious bird.

On the banks of the Hunter River this Kingfisher resorts to a very curious method of obtaining food. There is a kind of ant which builds a mud nest upon the dead branches and stems of the gum-trees, and by the unpractised eye would be taken for fungi or natural excrescences. The Kingfisher, however, knows better, and speedily demolishes the walls with its powerful beak, for the purpose of feeding upon the ants and their larvæ.

AUSTRALIAN KINGFISHER.

Hálcyon Sancta.

Like the preceding bird, the Australian Kingfisher is a most noisy creature, and remarkably fond of exercising its loud startling cry, which is said to resemble the shriek of a human being in distress, sharp, short, urgent, and frequently repeated. There is hardly any real nest in this species, which chooses a convenient hollow branch or "spout" as its home, and there lays its eggs. They are generally from three to five in number, and are of a pure white.

SPOTTED KINGFISHER.—*Céryle guttáta.*

The Spotted Kingfisher lives in India, where it is called by the natives by the name of Muchee-bag, or Fish-Tiger. It is a large bird, about fifteen inches in length, with a bill three inches long, and is remarkable as making a nest of mud, lined with grass, and placed among large stones. The eggs are four in number.

The chest and sides of the neck of the Fish-tiger are of a beautiful greyish-white, which slightly deepens into a very pale fawn on the abdomen and the under tail-coverts. The remainder of the body is covered with jetty-black plumage, relieved by numerous spots of pure white, and the head is decorated with a large and noble-looking crest, composed of elongated feathers of the same boldly contrasting hues. A few black spots form a curved line between the bill and the shoulder, and are scattered under the breast.

KINGFISHER.—*Alcédo Ispida*.

THE common KINGFISHER is very plentiful upon the banks of all English streams, where it may be seen darting along the course of the stream like a blue meteor, or sitting upon a branch or stump overhanging the water, and darting down every now and then into the stream upon its prey. When it has caught a fish it carries it ashore, generally beats it once or twice upon the ground, throws it up in the air, catches it with its head downwards and swallows it whole.

Sometimes the bird has been known to meet with a deadly retribution on the part of his prey, and to fall a victim to his voracity. One such example I have seen. A Kingfisher had caught a common bull-head, or miller's thumb, a well-known large-headed fish, and on attempting to swallow it had been baffled by the large head, which refused to pass through the gullet, and accordingly choked the bird. The Kingfisher must have been extremely hungry when it attempted to eat so large a morsel, as the fish was evidently of a size that could not possibly have been accommodated in the bird's interior.

The nest of the Kingfisher is made in a hole in the side of the river bank, and is composed of a mass of fish bones which are ejected from the stomach. This curious nest is about the size of a small saucer, and is extremely shallow, the hollow being hardly half an inch in depth. There is a fine specimen in the British Museum. The eggs are about eight in number, very round, and of a pinky white.

PARADISE JACAMAR.—*Gálbula Paradisea.*

GREEN JACAMAR.—*Galbula Viridis.*

The Jacamars are natives of the New World, and are beautifully coloured with green, purple, red, violet, and white. In their habits they are not unlike the trogons and flycatchers, seldom troubling themselves to chase their prey through the air, but preferring to sit upon a bough, watching the butterflies as they pass unconsciously near the feet of their destroyers, and then pounce suddenly upon them and secure them in the long bill. So persevering are they in their watchfulness, and so strong in their attachment to the spot where they have taken up their residence, that the locality where they feed can readily be discovered on account of the wings, legs, and other uneatable portions of their prey, which they twist off and throw away before endeavouring to swallow their victim.

BEE-EATER.—*Merops apiaster*.

The Bee-Eater is a very handsome bird, its feathers being tinted with blue, green, chestnut, and black. It derives its name from its habit of eating bees and other insects, being able to swallow them without damage from their stings.

Taking advantage of its insect-eating propensities, the boys of the Greek Archipelago, where the Bee-eater is very common, are in the habit of capturing it by means of a hook and line, in a kind of aërial angling, in which the atmosphere takes the place of water, and the victim is hauled struggling downwards, instead of being drawn struggling upwards. A hook is attached to the end of a strong but slender line, and fastened to a cicada or other insect, in such a manner as to cause no impediment to its flight, and the cicada is then allowed to fly about at will. The Bee-eater soon perceives its fluttering prey, and darting upon it with open beak, is caught by the hook and made prisoner.

While engaged in the pursuit of its prey, the Bee-eater flies at various heights, according to the weather and the species of insect which it is engaged in eating. Sometimes it may be seen careering high in air at so great an elevation that its beautiful colours cannot be distinguished, but attracting great admiration on account of its great command of wing and easy gliding movements. At another time it sweeps over the very surface of the ground, snapping up the bees, wasps, and other insects that are not in the habit of ascending to any great height.

AZURE-THROATED BEE-EATER.—*Nyctiornis Athertóni.*

The truly magnificent Azure-Throated Bee-eater is an inhabitant of India. It is a very rare bird on account of its extreme shyness, and the nature of the spot where it makes its residence. The home of this bird is always in the recesses of Indian forests, and in spite of its glowing colours and noisy tongue, it is so fearful of man that it is seldom seen. When discovered, however, it often falls an easy prey to the hunter on account of extreme nervousness. The report of a gun will have such an effect upon its nervous system as to stun it, and it sometimes happens that in the great hunting expeditions of the native chiefs, this Bee-eater is so stupified by the fire-arms, that it lies helplessly on the branch, and permits itself to be taken by hand.

The Azure-throated Bee-eater is a splendid bird, and is chiefly remarkable for the long soft azure feathers which hang from the throat and neck. The top of its head is bright scarlet and blue, and the upper surface a brilliant green.

RIFLE-BIRD.—*Ptilóris Paradiseus.*

The Slender Billed Birds always have a long and slender beak, sometimes curved and sometimes straight, delicate legs and long toes.

The Rifle-Bird lives in Australia, and is one of the most beautiful birds of that country, with the bright emerald green of the head and throat, and the velvet black of the body.

In size the Rifle-Bird is equal to a large pigeon, and in spite of its beauty it is not very often seen, as it is retiring in its habits, and seems to be confined to a very limited range of country. As far as it is at present known, it is found only in the thick "bush" of the south-eastern portions of Australia, and even there appears to be a very local bird. It is no wanderer, never flying to any great distance from its home, and procuring its food in the neighbourhood of its nest.

The habits of this bird are very like those of the common creeper of England, for it is generally seen upon the trunks and large branches of trees, running nimbly round them in a spiral course and extracting the insects on which it feeds from the crevices and recesses of the bark.

The general colour of this bird when full grown is velvety black above, and very deep olive below. The crown of the head and front of the throat are covered with little round scaly feathers of intense green. When young the bird is simply brown.

GOULD'S NEOMORPHA.—*Neomorpha Gouldii.*

The Neomorpha, another Australian bird, is remarkable on account of the bill, which is straight in the male, and much curved in the female. Mr. Gould describes its habits as follows:—

"These fine birds can only be obtained with the help of a native, who calls them with a shrill and long-continued whistle, resembling the sound of the native name of the species. After an extensive journey in the hilly forest in search of them, I had at last the pleasure of seeing four alight on the lower branches of the tree near which the native accompanying me stood. They came quick as lightning, descending from branch to branch, spreading out the tail and throwing up the wings. Anxious to obtain them, I fired; but they generally come so near that the natives kill them with sticks. Their food consists of seeds and insects."

TWELVE-THREAD PLUME BIRD.—*Epimachus albus.*

The beautiful Plume Birds are remarkable for the curious shape and brilliant colourings of their feathers, which in some places glow with a fire and lustre surpassing that of polished gems, and in others, are of the most delicate softness.

The Twelve-thread Plume Bird is a native of New Guinea, and is called on account of the twelve thread-like feathers which project from the plumage.

The general colour of the Twelve-thread Plume Bird is rich violet, so intense as to become black in some lights, and having always a velvet-like depth of tone. Around the neck is placed a collar of emerald-green feathers, which stand boldly from the neck, and present a most brilliant contrast with the deep violet of the back and wings. The tail is short in comparison with the dimensions of the bird. From the back and the rump spring a number of long silken plumes of a snowy white colour, and a loose downy structure that causes them to wave gracefully in the air at the slightest breeze.

HOOPOE.—*Upúpa Epops*.

The Hoopoe has long been celebrated for the beautiful feather-crest on its head, which can be raised or depressed at will. It is an English bird, but not very common.

The name Hoopoe is doubly appropriate to this bird, as it may be either derived from the crest (*huppe*), or from the peculiar sound which the bird is fond of uttering, and which resembles the syllable *hoop! hoop!* which, as Mr. Yarrell observes, "is breathed out so softly, yet rapidly, as to remind the hearer of the note of the dove." The pace of the Hoopoe is a tripping kind of walk, which is at times very quick and vivacious, and sometimes is slow and stately as if the bird were mightily proud of its crested head. When at liberty it is generally found in sequestered spots, preferring low, marshy grounds, and the vicinity of woods, because in these places it is certain to find plenty of food.

The food of the Hoopoe is almost entirely of an insect nature, although the bird will frequently vary its diet with tadpoles and other small creatures. Beetles and their larvæ, caterpillars and grubs of all kinds, are a favourite food with the Hoopoe, which displays much ingenuity in digging them out of the decayed wood in which they are often found.

FIERY-TAILED SUN-BIRD.—*Nectarínia ignicauda.*

The Sun-Birds are natives of the Old World, and in many of their habits are very like the humming-birds of the New World, decked with brilliant plumage, and feeding on honey, but not by hovering over a flower and sweeping up its nectar with the tongue, as is the case among the humming-birds. The Sun-Birds generally, if not always, perch before they attempt to feed, and flit restlessly from flower to flower, probing the blossoms in rapid succession, and uttering continually a sharp, eager cry, that indicates the earnestness of their occupation. In accordance with their peculiar habits, the feet and legs are very much stronger than those of the humming-birds; their wings are shorter, rounder, and less powerful, and their plumage is not so closely set.

When taken young, the Sun-Birds are very susceptible of human influence, rapidly becoming tame, and learning to fly about the room and take their food from the hand of their owners with charming familiarity. It has already been mentioned that the Sun-Bird utters a shrill, sharp whistle, while engaged in seeking food. This, however, is not their only cry, as many of them possess considerable musical powers, their cry, although feeble, being sweet and agreeably modulated.

The Fiery-Tailed Sun-Bird is an Indian species, being found most plentifully in Nepâl and near the Himalayas. It is blue on the head, bright scarlet above, with a band of yellow across the lower part of the back; the ten middle feathers of the tail are vermillion, and the breast is golden yellow with a dash of crimson in the centre.

BLUE-HEADED HONEY-SUCKER.—*Nectarinia cyanocéphala.*

The BLUE-HEADED HONEY-SUCKER is an inhabitant of Brazil, where it is extremely common, and by the bright gorgeousness of its plumage, and the restless activity of its movements, adds much to the beauty of the wondrous scenery among which it dwells.

It is found over the whole of Brazil, and may always be found haunting the blossoming trees and plants, dashing to and fro with its glancing flight, hovering with tremulous wing over the flowers and plunging its long beak eagerly into their newly-opened blossoms, where it finds its food.

It is not known to feed while on the wing, as is the case with the humming-birds, but perches near or upon the flower, and clings with its strong little feet while taking its meal.

The Blue-headed Honey-sucker derives its name from the azure-blue which decorates its head, and which is very changeable in different lights. The throat, the back, the tail, and the wings are black, except that the quill-feathers are edged with blue.

The female bird does not possess the beautiful tints of her mate, the greater part of her plumage being green, tinged with blue upon the head and the scapularies; the throat is grey. This bird is kown by several other titles, such as the Cayenne Warbler, the Blue-headed Warbler, and the Blue-headed Creeper.

GARRULOUS HONEY-EATER.—*Myzantha gárrula.*

The Garrulous Honey-eater is a native of Australia, and derives its name from its noisy conduct.

In its habits the Garrulous Honey-eater is very amusing, although it often is the cause of no small annoyance to the traveller or the sportsman, as will be seen by the following remarks made by Gould in his "Birds of Australia." "The Garrulous Honey-eater," he says, "is not gregarious, but moves about in small flocks of from five to ten in number. In disposition it is unlike any other bird I ever met with, for if its haunts be in the least intruded upon, it becomes the most restless and inquisitive creature possible, and withal so bold and noisy that it is regarded as a nuisance rather than an object of interest.

No sooner does the hunter come within the precincts of its abode, than the whole troop assemble round him, and perform the most grotesque actions, spreading out their wings and tails, hanging from the branches in every possible variety of position, and sometimes suspended by one leg; keeping up all the time one incessant babbling note. Were this only momentary, or for a short time, their droll attitudes and singular notes would be rather amusing than otherwise; but when they follow you through the entire forest, leaping and flying from branch to branch, and almost buffeting the dogs, they become very troublesome and annoying, awakening, as they do, the suspicions of the other animals of which you are in pursuit."

PÖE BIRD.—*Prosthemadéra Novæ Zeelándiæ.*

Among this group of birds the Pöe Bird, or Tue, or 'Parson Bird,' is one of the most conspicuous, being nearly as remarkable for its peculiar colouring as the rifle bird itself, although the hues of the feathers are not quite so resplendently brilliant as in that creature.

The Pöe Bird is a native of New Zealand, where it is far from uncommon, and is captured by the natives for the purpose of sale. Many individuals are brought over to Sydney, where, according to Dr. Bennett, they are kept in cages, and are very amusing in their habits, being easily domesticated and becoming very familiar with those who belong to the household. Independently of its handsome and rather peculiar colour, which make it very effective in a room, it possesses several other qualifications which render it a very desirable inhabitant of an aviary. Its native notes are very rich, the bird being considered a remarkably fine songster, and it also possesses the power of mimicking in a degree surpassing that of the common magpie or raven, and hardly yielding even to the famous mocking-bird himself. It learns to speak with great accuracy and fluency, and imitates any sound that may reach its ear, being especially successful in its reproduction of the song of other birds.

While at liberty in its native land it is remarkable for its quick, restless activity, as it flits rapidly about the branches, pecking here and there at a stray insect, diving into the recesses of a newly opened flower, and continually uttering its shrill sharp whistle.

The very quaint, and rather grotesque bird which is represented in the accompanying illustration is an inhabitant of Australia, and is very common in the southern parts of that continent, although at present it has not been seen in Van Diemen's Land.

By the colonists it is known by a variety of names, some relating to its aspect and others to its voice. Thus, it is named the FRIAR BIRD because the bare, oddly shaped head, with its projecting knob upon the forehead, is considered as resembling the bare shaven poll of the ancient friar. Another analogous name is the MONK BIRD. Another name is LEATHER-HEAD, a title which refers to the dark leathery aspect of the whole head, which is as stiff in outline and as dark in colour during life as after death. On account of its peculiar voice, it is also known by the names of "PIMLICO," "POOR-SOLDIER," or "FOUR-O'CLOCK," as its cry is said to resemble these words. The resemblance, however, cannot be very close, as neither of the words which it is supposed to utter could be mistaken for the other, so that the Friar Bird cannot be remarkable for the distinctness of its articulation.

FRIAR BIRD.—*Tropidorhynchus corniculátus.*

By the natives it is called Coldong.

The Friar Bird is very talkative, delighting to get upon the topmost branch of some lofty tree, and there chatter by the hour together at the top of its loud and peculiar voice, as if it were desirous of attracting attention to its powers. Among the branches it is extremely active, traversing them in all directions with great ease, and clinging to their rough bark by the grasp of its powerful toes and curved claws.

BRUSH WATTLE BIRD.

Anthochæra carunculáta.

The Brush-Wattle Bird is spread over the whole of Southern Australia, and is one of the best known of the birds belonging to that country. It may generally be found upon lofty trees, and, like others of the same group, especially haunts the gum trees for the purpose of feeding upon the juices of the flowers. It always chooses the most recently opened blossoms, as they are not so likely to be rifled of their sweet stores as those which have been exposed to the attacks of the honey-eating insects and birds. The method of feeding is the same as that which is pursued by the other Honey-eaters, viz. by plunging the long bill and slender tongue into the very depths of the blossoms, and brushing out their contents. It has a great affection for the flowers of the Banksia, and is sure to be found wherever these plants are in blossom, thereby doing good service to the intending purchaser of land; for the Banksia always grows upon poor soil, so that, according to Mr. Gould, the cry of this bird warns the settler not to buy the land on which it is heard.

It is extremely active and quick of foot among the branches, running about the boughs in any position, and seeming to care nothing whether its back or head be downwards or upwards. It is a lively, restless creature, ever on the move, tripping over the branches with a quick, easy step, examining every flower, diving its long tongue into its recesses and flying quickly from tree to tree as fancy may dictate.

The wonderful little Humming-Birds, which contain the very smallest as well as the most gorgeously coloured of the feathered tribes, are natives of the New World; and in many places, especially in Central America and the neighbouring islands, are very common. Mostly they love the hot regions, but, in some instances, they are found on the tops of lofty mountains, just on the line of perpetual snow.

They have very long tongues, which can be thrust out to a considerable distance, and enable the bird either to lick the sweet juices from flowers, or to capture the tiny insects which love to congregate at the bottom of honey-bearing blossoms.

It is only the male who possesses the beautiful colours, the females being sober and simple in their plumage.

The WHITE-BOOTED RACKET-TAIL is found on the Columbian Andes, at a great elevation. It is a wonderful bird, on account of the long tail feathers with their racket-like tips. While the bird is flying through the air these feathers wave about in a most graceful manner. The flight is swift and straight, like an arrow shot from a bow.

WHITE-BOOTED RACKET-TAIL.

Spathúra Underwoodii.

Male and Female.

There are several species belonging to this genus, among which may be mentioned the PERUVIAN RACKET-TAIL, a bird which may be distinguished by the rusty-red colour of the leg-muffs.

SALLE'S HERMIT HUMMING-BIRD.—*Phaëthornis Augusti.*

ALL the HERMIT HUMMING-BIRDS are remarkable for the very long and beautifully graduated tail, all the feathers being long and pointed, and the two central far exceeding the rest. The two sexes are mostly alike, both in the colour and shape of their plumage and in size. These birds inhabit Venezuela and the Carracas, being generally found in the richest district of those localities, where the flowers blossom most abundantly.

All the Hermits build a very curious and beautiful nest, of a long funnel-like form tapering to a slender point, and woven with the greatest neatness to some delicate twig or pendent leaf by means of certain spiders' webs. The material of which it is made is silky cotton fibre, intermixed with a woolly kind of furze, and bound together with spider-web.

Our present example is SALLE'S HERMIT, a most beautiful bird. Very little is known of its habits, but, like the generality of Humming-birds, it does not possess any great power of voice. Indeed, even in the few instances where one of these birds is gifted with vocal powers, its song is of a feeble and uncertain character, and in England would attract little attention.

The plumage of this bird on the upper parts of its body are green-bronze, excepting the upper tail coverts, which are rusty red. The wings are purple-brown. The central tail-feathers are bronze, largely tipped with white, and the remaining feathers are white, with the exception of a broad black band, drawn obliquely across them near the base. Above and below the eye there is a white streak, and the colour of the under parts of the body is sober grey.

SICKLE-BILL HUMMING BIRD.—*Eutoxeres A'quila*.

SEVERAL species are called SICKLE-BILLS, on account of the peculiar form of their beaks, which are rather long, and sharply curved like a common sickle. This kind of beak is useful in order to suit the shape of the flowers on which the bird feeds.

This SICKLE-BILL is a native of Veragua and Bogotá, and is very rare even in the countries which it inhabits.

The plumage is not very brilliant in its hues, but the various tints with which it is coloured are pleasing in their arrangement, and give to the bird a very pretty aspect.

The crown of its head and the little crest are blackish brown, and each feather has one small spot of buff on its tip. The upper parts of the body are of a dark shining green, with a slight buffy wash, and on the tips of several of the secondaries there is a little white spot. The two central feathers of the tail are a dark glossy green with small white tips, and the others are of the same hue in their outer webs, greenish brown on the inner, and largely tipped with white. The under surface is brownish-black, diversified with some dark buff streaks upon the throat and breast, and with white streaks upon the abdomen and flanks; the under tail-coverts are brown fringed with buff. The total length of the bird is about four and a half inches.

SNOW-CAP HUMMING-BIRD.—*Microchæra albocoronáta.*

SPANGLED COQUETTE.—*Lophornis Regínæ.*

The Little Snow-cap is one of the rarest among the Humming-birds. It lives in New Granada, and the person who discovered it gave the following account of it:—

"The first one I saw was perched on a twig, pluming its feathers. I was doubtful for a few moments whether so small an object could be a bird, but on close examination I convinced myself of the fact and secured it. Another I encountered while bathing, and for a time I watched its movements before shooting it. The little creature would poise itself about three feet or so above the surface of the water, and then as quick as thought dart downwards, so as to dip its miniature head in the placid pool; then up again to its original position, quite as quickly as it had descended. These movements of darting up and down it would repeat in rapid succession, which produced not a moderate disturbance of the surface of the water for such a diminutive creature. After a considerable number of dippings, it alighted on a twig near at hand, and commenced pluming its feathers."

On the same drawing may be seen another remarkable little bird, possessed of a most beautiful and graceful crest. This is the Spangled Coquette. All the Coquettes possess a well-defined crest upon the head, and a series of projecting feathers from the neck.

The Spangled Coquette is a native of several parts of Columbia, and was first brought to England in 1847. The singular crest is capable of being raised or depressed at the will of the bird.

SAPPHO COMET.—*Cométes sparganúrus.*

YARRELL'S WOODSTAR.—*Calothórax Yarrellii.*

The Sappho Comet lives in Bolivia, and is a wonderfully beautiful bird, the upper parts of the body being bright green, the lower part of the back crimson, and the tail feathers rich fiery red, tipped with velvety black.

The Yarrell's Woodstar is also a Bolivian bird, and is remarkable for the arrangement of the tail feathers.

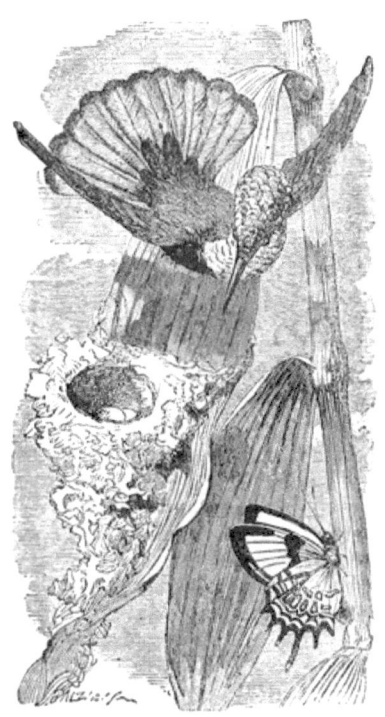

RUBY AND TOPAZ
HUMMING-BIRD.

Chrysolampis moschitus.

The Ruby and Topaz Humming-bird derives its name from the colouring of its head and throat, the former being of a deep ruby tint, and the latter of a resplendent topaz.

Sometimes it is called the Ruby-headed Humming-bird, and it is also known under the name of the Aurora.

It is very common in Bahia, the Guianas, Trinidad and the Caraccas, and as it is in great request for the dealers, is killed by thousands annually.

There is no species so common in ornamental cases of Humming-birds as the Ruby and Topaz.

It makes a very beautiful nest, round, cup-like, and delicately woven of cotton and various fibres, and covered externally with little leaves and bits of lichen.

This nest is fastened to a long, drooping leaf, in a very ingenious manner, and is, by its peculiar position, protected from some of the many enemies which always surround birds while engaged in the duties of bringing up a family.

It is a lovely little creature, the ruby of the head, and topaz of the throat, contrasting boldly with the rich, deep velvety brown of the back.

The plumage of this species is extremely variable, but may be described briefly as follows:—The forehead, the crown, and the nape of the neck are metallic ruby red, and the chin, throat, and chest are effulgent topaz. The upper parts of the body are velvety bronze-brown, and the wings are purple-brown. The tail is rich chestnut-red, tipped with black, and the abdomen is a dark olive-brown. The female has none of the ruby patches on the head, but retains a little of the topaz on the throat.

VERVAIN HUMMING-BIRD.—*Mellisuga minima.*

The beautiful little Vervain Humming-bird is one of the minutest examples of feathered life at present known to zoologists. In total length this bird does not measure three inches; while, as the tail occupies nearly an inch and the head half an inch, the actual length of the body will be seen to be not quite an inch and a half. It is a native of Jamaica, and has been admirably described by Mr. Gosse, while treating of the birds which inhabit that island.

The name of Vervain Humming-bird has been given to this tiny creature, because it is in the habit of feeding on the blossoms of the West Indian Vervain.

This little bird has a pleasant but not powerful voice, of which Mr. Bullock writes as follows:—

"He had taken his station on the twig of a tamarind-tree which was close to the barn and overspread part of the yard; there, perfectly indifferent to the number of persons constantly passing within a few yards, he spent most of the day. There were few blossoms on the tree, and it was not the breeding season, yet he most pertinaciously kept absolute possession of his domain; for the moment any other bird, though ten times as large as himself, approached near his tree, he attacked it most furiously and drove it off, always returning to the same twig he had before occupied, and which he had worn quite bare for three or four inches by constantly feeding on it. I often approached within a few feet with pleasure, observing his tiny operations of cleaning and pluming, and listening to his weak, simple, and oft-repeated note. I could easily have caught him, but was unwilling to destroy so interesting a little visitant, who had afforded me so much pleasure.

OVEN BIRD.—*Furnárius fuliginósus.*

WE now leave the humming-birds and come to the creepers.

The OVEN-BIRDS derive their name from the peculiar form of their nest.

The edifice, for it fully deserves that name, is of considerable dimensions when compared with the small size of its architect, and is built in the shape of a dome, the entrance being on one side, so as to present a decided resemblance to an ordinary oven. The walls of the nest are fully an inch in thickness, and the materials of which the structure is composed are clay, grass, and various kinds of vegetable substances, which are woven and plastered together in so workmanlike a manner, that the nest is quite hard and firm when the clay has been dried in the sun. The bird seems to be conscious of the security of its nest, for it takes no pains to conceal its habitation, but builds openly upon some exposed spot, such as the large leafless branch of a tree, the top of palings, or even the interior of houses or barns.

The Oven-bird is a bold little creature, caring nothing for the close proximity of man, and attacking fiercely any other bird that might happen to approach too closely to its residence, screeching defiantly the while. It is a quick, active bird, tripping over the ground with great rapidity while searching after its prey, and is almost invariably found in company with its mate.

The Oven-bird is not content with barely building this curious domed structure, but adds to its security by separating it into two parts, by means of a partition reaching nearly to the roof, the eggs being placed in the inner chamber.

The bed on which the eggs are placed consists mostly of feathers and soft grasses. The number of the eggs is generally about four.

ANOTHER very small group of the Creepers is represented by the CURVED-BILLED CREEPER, a bird about the size of an English blackbird, which is found in the forests of Brazil.

It is chiefly remarkable from the curiously-formed beak, which is very long in proportion to the size of the bird, and is curved in a manner that can best be understood by reference to the engraving. The bill, although so much elongated, is possessed of considerable strength, and is evidently employed for the purpose of drawing the insects on which the creature feeds from the crevices of the bark in which they dwell.

As is indicated by the stiff and sharply-pointed feathers of the tail, the Curved-billed Creeper is in the habit of traversing the trunks of trees, and is able to support itself in a perpendicular position by hooking its long curved claws into the inequalities of the bark, and resting the weight of its body upon the stiff tail feathers.

The general colour of this bird is brown, with a wash of cinnamon upon the greater part of of the surface. The head and neck are of a greyer brown, and spotted with white

CURVED-BILLED CREEPER.

Dendrocolaptes procurvus.

COMMON TREE-CREEPER.

Cérthia familiáris.

The COMMON TREE-CREEPER is one of the best known British birds, and is one of the prettiest and most interesting of the feathered tribes that are found in this country. It is a very small bird, hardly so large as a sparrow, and beautifully slender in shape. The bill is rather long, pointed, and curved, and the tail-feathers are stiff and pointed at their extremities. The food of the Creeper consists chiefly of insects, although the bird will sometimes vary its diet by seeds and other vegetable substances. The insects on which it feeds live principally under the bark of various rough-skinned trees, and when it is engaged in running after its food, it runs spirally up the trunk with wonderful ease and celerity, probing every crevice with ready adroitness, its whole frame instinct with sparkling eagerness, and its little black eyes glancing with the exuberance of its delight. While running on the side of the tree which is nearest to the spectator, it presents a very curious appearance, as its dark-brown back and quick tripping movements give it a great resemblance to a mouse, and ever and anon, as it comes again into sight from the opposite side of the trunk, its beautifully white breast gleams suddenly in contrast with the sombre-coloured bark. Its eyes are wonderfully keen, as it will discern insects of so minute a form that the human eye can hardly perceive them, and it seems to possess some instinctive mode of detecting the presence of its insect prey beneath moss or lichens, and will perseveringly bore through the substance in which they are hidden, never failing to secure them at last.

The Creeper is a very timid bird, and if it is alarmed at the sight of a human being, it will either fly off to a distant tree, or will quietly slip round the trunk of the tree on which it is running and keep itself carefully out of sight. It soon, however, gains confidence, and, provided that the spectator remains perfectly still, the little head and white breast may soon be seen peering anxiously round the trunk, and in a few minutes the bird will resume its progress upon the tree and run cheerily up the bark, accompanying itself with its faint trilling song. It seldom attempts a long flight, seeming to content itself with flitting from tree to tree.

THE COMMON NUTHATCH is also very plentiful in England. Although by no means a rare bird, it is seldom seen except by those who are acquainted with its haunts, on account of its shy and retiring habits. As it feeds mostly on nuts, it is seldom seen except in woods or their immediate vicinity, although it will sometimes become rather bold and frequent gardens and orchards where nuts are grown. The bird also feeds upon insects, which it procures, from under the bark after the manner of the

NUTHATCH—*Sitta Europæa.*

creepers, and it is not unlikely that many of the nuts which are eaten by the Nuthatch have been inhabited by the grub of the nut weevil. It will also feed upon the seeds of different plants, especially preferring those which it pecks out of the fur-cones. Beech mast also seems grateful to its palate, and it will occasionally take to eating fruit.

In order to extract the kernel of the nut, the bird fixes the fruit securely in some convenient crevice, and, by dint of repeated hammerings with its beak, breaks a large ragged hole in the shell, through which the kernel is readily extracted. The blows are not merely given by the stroke of the beak, but the bird grasps firmly with its strong claws, and swinging its whole body upon its feet delivers its stroke with the full weight and sway of the body.

The Nuthatch is a capital climber of tree-trunks, even surpassing the creeper in the agility with which it ascends and descends the perpendicular surface, clinging firmly with its strong claws, and running equally well whether head upwards or downwards. Even the creeper does not attempt to run down a tree with its head towards the ground. It is a very hardy bird, contriving to pick up an abundant supply of food even in the depths of winter, always appearing plump and lively.

The colour of the Nuthatch is delicate bluish-grey, the throat is white, the under parts are reddish-brown, warming into rich chestnut on the flanks. From the angle of the mouth a narrow black band passes towards the back of the neck, enveloping the eye in its course, and terminating suddenly before it reaches the shoulders.

LYRE BIRD.—*Menura superba.*

STRANGE as it may seem, the large LYRE BIRD belongs to the family of the wrens. It is a native of Australia, where it is sometimes called the PHEASANT. It lives in the forests, and is very shy and watchful, so that it is not often seen, and it is so quick in its movements among the branches that it is not easily shot.

The common Wren is a very well known British bird. The Wren is seldom seen in the open country, and does not venture upon any lengthened flight, but confines itself to the hedgerows and brushwood, where it may often be observed hopping and skipping like a tiny feathered mouse among the branches. It especially haunts the hedges which are flanked by ditches, as it can easily hide itself in such localities, and can also obtain a plentiful supply of food. By remaining perfectly quiet, the observer can readily watch its movements, and it is really an interesting sight to see the little creature flitting about the brushwood, flirting its saucily expressive tail, and uttering its quick and cheering note.

The voice of the Wren is very sweet and melodious, and of a more powerful character than would be imagined from the dimensions of the bird.

WREN.—*Troglodýtes vulgáris.*

The Wren is a merry little creature, and chants its gay song on the slightest encouragement of weather. Even in winter there needs but the gleam of a few stray sunbeams to set the Wren singing, and the cold Christmas season is often cheered with its happy notes. While skipping among the branches, the Wren utters a continuous little twitter, which, although not worthy of being reckoned as a song, is yet very soft and pleasing.

The nest of the Wren is rather an ambitious structure, being a completely domed edifice, and built in a singularly ingenious manner. If, however, the bird can find a suitable spot, such as a hole in a decaying tree, the gnarled and knotted branches of old ivy, or the overhanging eaves of a deserted building, where a natural dome is formed, it is sure to seize upon the opportunity and to make a dome of very slight workmanship. The dome, however, always exists, and is composed of leaves and moss, and is very warm and comfortable. It is a very singular fact, that a Wren will often commence and partly build three or four nests in different localities before it settles finally upon one spot. Some persons have supposed that these supplementary nests are built by the parent bird as houses for its young after they have grown too large to be contained within the house where they were born, while others have suggested that they are experimental nests made by the inexperienced young while trying their 'prentice beak in the art of bird architecture.

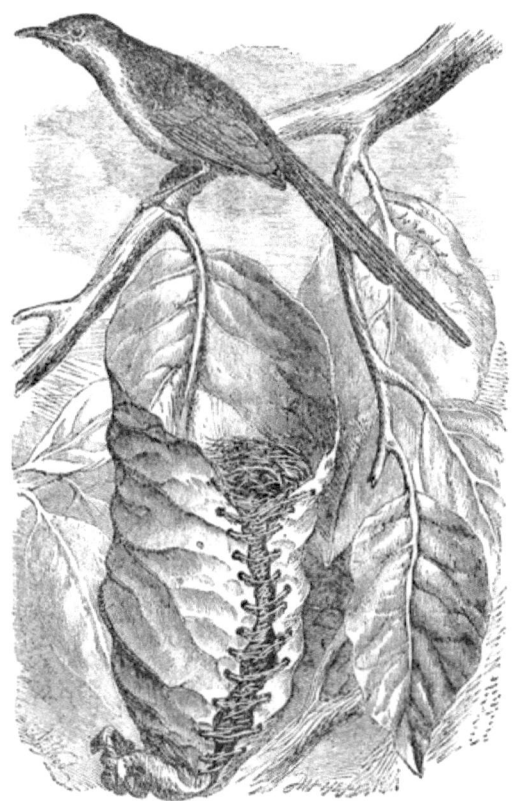

TAILOR-BIRD.—*Orthotómus longicaudus.*

The Warblers are numerous all over the world, and we have many examples in England.

The first example of the soft-tailed Warblers is the celebrated TAILOR-BIRD of India and the Indian Archipelago. There are many species of Tailor-birds and as they all possess similar habits, there is no need of describing more than the example which has been given. They are peculiar birds, haunting cultivated grounds, and being generally seen in pairs on fields and in gardens. They dislike lofty elevations, and may usually be noticed near the ground, hopping about the lower branches of trees and shrubs in their search after insects, and occasionally seeking their prey on the ground. Their flight is rapid but undulating, after the manner of many short-winged and long-tailed birds.

The Tailor-bird is a sober little creature, not more conspicuous than a common sparrow, and is chiefly remarkable for its curious nest, which is made in a singular and most ingenious manner. Taking two leaves at the extremity of a slender twig, the bird literally sews them together at their edges, its bill taking the place of the needle and vegetable fibres constituting the thread. A quantity of soft cottony down is then pushed between the leaves, and a convenient hollow scraped out in which the eggs may lie, and the young birds may rest at their ease. Sometimes, if the leaf be large enough, its two edges are drawn together, but in general a pair of leaves are needed. A few feathers are sometimes mixed with the down.

EMEU WREN.—*Stipiturus malachurus.*

Our last, and perhaps the most curious example of the soft-tailed birds, is the beautiful little Emeu Wren of Australia.

This pretty bird is remarkable for the development of the tail-feathers, which are extremely lengthened, and are nothing more than bare shafts slightly fringed on each side. The bird never perches on high trees, and very seldom takes to wing, but runs over the grass with very great rapidity, holding its tail erect over its back in a singularly pert manner. It is generally found among long grass, and, according to Dr. Bennett, it congregated some years since in the Sydney Domain, near the Botanic Gardens, but has not since appeared in that locality. The colour of this little bird is mottled brown above, and very light fawn below, deepening into chestnut on the flanks. The throat of the male is tinged with blue, and his tail-feathers are longer than those of his mate.

The nest of the Emeu Wren is very large in comparison with the size of its inhabitant, and is placed on the ground, where it looks like a large ball of grass with a hole in the side. The interior is snugly lined with soft feathers, and there are generally three eggs.

GOLDEN CRESTED WREN.—*Régulus cristátus.*

FIRE CRESTED WREN.—*Régulus ignicapillus*

The tiny Golden-crested Wren, as it is popularly called, is very common throughout England, and may be seen hopping and flitting merrily among the branches in copses, orchards, and plantations. Although from its diminutive size it has gained the title of Wren, it has no claim to that designation, and is more rightly termed the Kinglet or Regulus.

This "shadow of a bird," as it is happily called by White, in his "Natural History of Selborne," is a remarkably hardy little creature, braving the severest frosts of winter, and mostly disdaining to avail itself of the shelter of human habitations. On account of its minute proportions and its retiring habits, it is a very unobtrusive bird, and is often thought to be extremely rare in localities where it may be found plentifully by those who know where to look for it. In Derbyshire, for instance, it is held to be extremely scarce, but I always procure specimens at will by a judicious disposition of a little birdlime, and I have frequently discovered the admirably hidden and beautifully constructed nests of these interesting birds.

The Fire-crested Wren is very similar to the preceding species, but may be distinguished from it by the ruddy hue of the forehead, the fiery orange of the crest, and the decidedly yellow hue of the sides of the neck. It is an inhabitant of England, but is a rather rarer bird than the Golden-crest. Owing to the great resemblance between the two species, they have often been mistaken for each other, and it is only within a comparatively recent period that their diversity was established.

CHIFF-CHAFF, OR LESSER PETTICHAPS.—*Sylvia rufa.*
WILLOW WARBLER.—*Sylvia tróchilus.*

THE tiny CHIFF-CHAFF, one of the smallest of the British birds, is the first Warbler that makes its appearance in these islands, and that cheers us with its pretty little song and its light, lively actions.

The curious name of this bird has been derived from its cry, which bears some resemblance to the words " Chiff-chaff! Cherry-churry!" often repeated. This little song is sometimes uttered while the bird is on the wing, but generally when it is perched on some convenient bough of a lofty tree. The localities which it most frequents are woods and hedgerows, and so lively is it in temper, that its pleasant little voice is often heard before the trees have put forth their verdure. It is a very useful bird, as it feeds almost wholly on insects, and on its first arrival saves many a grand oak-tree from destruction by devouring the caterpillars of the well-known green oak moth, which roll up the leaves in so curious a manner and come tumbling out of their green houses at the slightest alarm. Gnats and other small flies are a diet much in favour with the Chiff-chaff.

Another interesting member of this large genus is the WILLOW WARBLER, WILLOW WREN, or YELLOW WREN, its various names being derived from the localities which it frequents and the colour of its feathers.

The habits of this bird are very like those of the Whitethroat, and it feeds on much the same kind of food, preferring insects to any other diet, and seldom if ever invading the fruit trees. It generally arrives in England about the middle of April, when its merry song may be heard enlivening the hedgerows and copses, sometimes being poured forth while the bird is on wing, but generally from some elevated branch.

BLACKCAP WARBLER.—*Sylvia atricapilla.*

With the exception of the nightingale, the Blackcap Warbler is the sweetest and richest toned of all the British song-birds, and in many points the voice of the Blackcap is even superior.

The Blackcap derives its name from the tuft of dark feathers which crown the head, and which in the males are coal black, but in the female a deep reddish-brown.

While singing, the Blackcap chooses some spot where it can conceal itself if alarmed, and there pour forth its melodious notes in security. Sometimes he will sing while perched upon an open branch, but he is very jealous of spectators, and if he fancies himself visible, immediately drops among the foliage and is lost to sight. The song of this bird is well described by Mr. Mudie in the following words :—

"Its song is generally given from a high perch or an elevated branch, on the top twig if the tree be not very lofty. While it sings, the axis of the body is very oblique by the elevation of the head, and the throat is much inflated. While the bird is trilling, in which it excels every songster of the grove in rapidity and clearness, and in the swells and cadences which it gives to the same trill, the throat has a very convulsive motion, and the whole bird appears to be worked into a high state of excitement."

The nest of the Blackcap is generally placed only a foot or so above the ground, within the shelter of a dense bush or tuft of rank herbage, and is composed of vegetable fibres and hairs rather loosely put together. The eggs are four or five in number, and are of a pale reddish-brown dappled with a deeper hue of brown. The general colour of the Blackcap is grey, with a wash of dark green upon the upper surface and ashen grey upon the lower surface.

NIGHTINGALE.—*Luscinia Philoméla.*

The well-known and far-famed Nightingale is, happily for us, an inhabitant of England, visiting us about the middle of April and remaining until the breeding season is over.

As is well known, the song of the Nightingale is mostly uttered in the evening, but the bird may sometimes be heard in full song throughout the day.

Towards the end of June, when the young birds are hatched, the song changes into a kind of rough croaking sound, which is uttered by the way of warning, and accompanied with a sharp snapping sound of the beak. The time when the Nightingales sing loudest and most constantly is during the week or two after their arrival, for they are then engaged in attracting their mates, and sing in fierce rivalry of each other, hoping to fascinate their brides by the splendour of their voices. When once the bird has procured a partner, he becomes deeply attached to her, and if he should be captured, soon pines away and dies, full of sorrowful remembrances. The bird dealers are therefore anxious to catch the Nightingale before the first week has elapsed, as they can then, by dint of care and attention, preserve the bird in full song to a very late period.

The colour of the Nightingale is a rich hair-brown upon the upper parts of the body, and greyish-white below, the throat being of a lighter hue than the breast and abdomen. The entire length of the bird rather exceeds six inches.

WHINCHAT.—*Pratincola rubétra.*   STONECHAT.—*Pratincola rubicola.*

The Whinchat is tolerably common in England, and may be found among furze and stony ground. It is a prettily marked bird, mottled above with brown and white, and fawn below.

Like the wheatear, the Whinchat becomes extremely fat in the autumn, and as it is prized as a delicacy for the table, is rather persecuted by the game-dealers and their assistants. The food of this bird is the same as that of the stonechat. The Whinchat arrives in this country about the middle or towards the end of April, according to the locality and the weather. It builds its nest soon after its arrival, and hatches its young about the end of May or the beginning of June. The nest is placed on the ground, is made after the fashion of the stonechat's habitation, and contains from four to six bluish-green eggs, slightly speckled with reddish-brown.

The Stonechat is one of the birds that remain in England throughout the year, being seen during the winter months among the furze-covered commons which are now rapidly becoming extinct.

The name of Chat is earned by the bird in consequence of its extreme volubility, for it is one of the noisiest birds in existence. Its song is low and sweet, and may be heard to great advantage, as the bird is not at all shy, and, trusting to its powers of concealment, sings merrily until the spectator has approached within a short distance, and then, dropping among the furze, glides quickly through the prickly maze, and rises at some distance ready to renew its little song.

REDSTART.—*Ruticilla phœnicura.*

The Redstart is well known by its black chin, and the light ruddy feathers on the lower part of the back. It is an elegantly shaped bird, and a great ornament to our fields and hedgerows. The name of Redstart is a very appropriate one, and has been given to the bird in allusion to the peculiar character of its flight. While walking quietly along the hedgerows, the observer may often see a bird flash suddenly out of the leaves, flirt its tail in the air, displaying strongly a bright gleam of ruddy hue, and after a sharp dash of a few yards, turn into the hedge again with as much suddenness as it had displayed in its exit. These manœuvres it will repeat frequently, always keeping well in front, and at last it will quietly slip through the hedge, double back on the opposite side, and return to the spot from whence it had started.

No one need fancy, from seeing the bird in the hedge, that its nest is in close proximity, for the Redstart seldom builds in such localities, only haunting them for the sake of obtaining food for its young. The nest is almost invariably built in the hole of an old wall, in a crevice of rock, a heap of large stones, in a hollow tree, or in very thick ivy. The eggs are generally five in number, although they vary from four to seven, and are of a beautiful blue, with a slight tinge of green. They are not unlike those of the common hedge sparrow, but are shorter and of a different shape.

The Redstart has a very sweet song, which bears some resemblance to that of the nightingale.

REDBREAST.—*Erythacus rubécula.*

There are few birds which are more familiar to us than the Redbreast or Robin, a bird which is woven among our earliest recollections, through the medium of the Children in the Wood, and the mournful ballad of the Death and Burial of Poor Cock Robin.

Although the Redbreast remains in England throughout the winter, it is very susceptible to cold, and one of the first birds to seek for shelter, its appearance among the outhouses being always an indication of coming inclemency. In cold weather, the Redbreast seldom perches upon twigs and branches, but crouches in holes, or sits upon the ground. The bird seems strongly attached to man and his home, and will follow the ploughman over the fields, picking up the worms which he turns up with the ploughshare, or enter his house and partake of his evening meal. Both bold and shy, the Redbreast is a most engaging bird, and seldom fails of receiving the affection of those to whom he attaches himself. One of these birds was exceedingly familiar with all our family, his acquaintance having commenced through the medium of some crumbs from our hands, and would always come to us whenever we called his name, "Bobby." Sometimes he would accompany us on our way to church through the lanes, and I have even seen him keeping pace with us along the one-sided street of Oxford, that is appropriately named Long Wall.

While hopping and feeding about the ground, it is wonderful to see what large worms and insects the little bird will devour. Should the worm be too large for him to swallow entire, as indeed is mostly the case, he tosses it about with his beak, bangs it against the ground, flings it over his head, jumps on it, and when he has thus mashed it into a pulp, pulls it to bits, and devours it piecemeal.

The colour of the male Robin is bright olive-brown on the back, orange-red on the throat, chin, breast, forehead, and round the eye. A stripe of blue-grey runs round the red, and the abdomen and lower part of the breast are white. The bill and eyes are black.

HEDGE SPARROW, OR ACCENTOR.—*Accentor modularius.*

The Hedge Accentor is very common through the whole of England, and may be heard in the gardens, copses, and hedge-rows, chanting its pleasing and plaintive melody without displaying much fear of its auditors. It seems, indeed, to be actually attracted to man, and, in spite of the terrible havoc which is made year after year by young bird-nesters among its homes, it always draws near to human habitations as soon as the cold days of autumn commence, and may be seen flitting about the barns and outhouses in a perfectly unconcerned manner.

It is especially adapted for living among the hedges, as it possesses a singular facility in threading its way through the twigs, stems, and branches. It seems equally at home in dried brushwood, and may often be seen traversing the interior of a woodpile with perfect ease. The nest is one of the earliest to be built, and it is frequently completed and the eggs laid before the leaves have shown themselves.

The song of the Hedge Accentor is sweet, but not varied nor powerful, and has a peculiar plaintive air about it. The bird is a persevering songster, continuing to sing throughout a large portion of the year, and only ceasing during the time of the ordinary moult. Like many other warbling birds, it possesses considerable powers of imitation, and can mock with some success the greater number of British song-birds.

GREAT TITMOUSE.—*Parus major*.

The Titmice are curious little birds, with strong short bills and very active habits. Several kinds of Titmice inhabit England, of which the Great Titmouse is the largest.

It does not emigrate, finding a sufficiency of winter food in its native land. During the summer it generally haunts the forests, gardens, or shrubberies, and may be seen hopping and running about the branches of the trees in a most adroit manner, searching for insects, and occasionally knocking them out of their hiding-places by sharp blows of the bill. The beak of the Great Titmouse is, although so small, a very formidable one, for the creature has often been known to set upon the smaller birds, and to kill them by repeated blows on the head, afterwards pulling the skull to pieces, and picking out the brains.

During the winter, the Great Titmouse draws near to human habitations, and by foraging among the barns and outhouses, seldom fails in discovering an ample supply of food.

The nest of the Great Titmouse is always made in some convenient hollow, generally that of a tree, but often in the holes of old walls, and in the cavities that are formed by thick gnarled roots in the sides of a bank. Hollow trees, however, are the favourite nesting-places of this bird, which is able to shape the hollow to its liking, by chiselling away the decayed wood with its sharp, strong beak. The materials of which the nest is made vary according to the locality. Should the hollow be a deep and warm one, the bird takes very little trouble about the nest, merely bringing a few feathers and mosses as a soft bed on which to place the eggs. If, however, the locality be more exposed, the Titmouse builds a regular nest of moss, hair, and feathers, in which to lay its eggs. There are generally from eight to twelve eggs in each nest, and their colour is whitish grey, covered with mottlings of a rusty red, which are thickly gathered towards the larger end.

This bird is ashy green above, yellow below, and with a black head and throat.

The little BLUE TITMOUSE is one of the most familiar birds of England, as it is widely spread throughout the land, and is of so bold a nature that it exhibits itself fearlessly to any observer.

In many of its habits it resembles the last-mentioned species, but it nevertheless possesses a very marked character, and has peculiarities which are all its own. As it trips glancingly over the branches it hardly looks like a bird, for its quick limbs, and strong claws carry it over the twigs with such rapidity that it resembles a blue mouse rather than one of the feathered tribe.

BLUE TITMOUSE.—*Parus cœrúeus.*

Being almost exclusively an insect-eating bird, and a most voracious little creature, it renders invaluable service to the agriculturist and the gardener by discovering and destroying the insects which crowd upon the trees and plants in the early days of spring, and which, if not removed, would effectually injure a very large proportion of the fruit and produce. In the course of a single day a pair of blue Titmice were seen to visit their nest four hundred and seventy-five times, never bringing less than one large caterpillar, and generally two or three small ones. These birds, therefore, destroyed, on the average, upwards of five hundred caterpillars daily, being a minimum of fifteen thousand during the few weeks employed in rearing their young.

While searching for insects, the Blue Titmouse often bites away the buds of fruit trees, together with pears and apples, but in almost every case it seeks to devour, not the fruit, but a maggot which lies concealed within it, and which, if not destroyed, would not only injure the particular fruit, but would also destroy many others by means of its future progeny. The food of this bird is of a most multifarious character, for the Blue Titmouse has been known to eat eggs, other birds which it kills when young or disabled, meat of various kinds, for which it always haunts the knackers' yards and country slaughter-houses, peas, oats, and the various kinds of food which are to be found in farmyards. So fond is it of fat meat, that a piece of beef-suet is a bait which always succeeds in attracting the Titmouse into the jaws of the trap. It has even been known to peck holes in hens' eggs, for the purpose of eating the contents; but on account of the large size of the eggs, it was not able to attain its purpose. I have even seen the Titmice unite against a tame hawk which I kept, assault him, and carry off the piece of meat which had just been given to him.

THE two little birds which are represented in the accompanying illustration are among the most striking examples of this pretty group, the one for its bold and conspicuous crest, and the other for the curious colouring of the head and neck.

The YELLOW-CHEEKED TITMOUSE inhabits several parts of Asia, and is mostly found among the north-western Himalayas, where it is rather abundant. In its habits it resembles the ordinary Titmouse of Europe. The nest of this species is constructed of moss, hair, and fibres, and is lined softly with feathers. The position in which it is placed is usually a cavity at the bottom of some hollow stump, generally a decaying oak, and it contains four or five eggs of a delicate-white blotched with brownish spots. The colouring of this bird is rather peculiar and decidedly bold. The top of the head, the crest, a streak below the eye, and a broad band reaching from the chin to the extremity of the abdomen, are deep jetty black. The cheeks are light yellow, as is the whole of the under surface of the body, with the exception of the flanks, which take a greener hue. The wings are grey, mottled with black and white, and the tail is black with a slight edging of olive-green.

YELLOW-CHEEKED TITMOUSE.
Parus xanthógenys.

RUFOUS-BELLIED TITMOUSE.
Parus rubidiventris.

The RUFOUS-BELLIED TITMOUSE inhabits Southern India and Nepâl, and cannot be considered as a rare bird. In this pretty creature the head, the crest, and the throat are jet black, contrasting boldly with the pure white of the ear-coverts and the back of the neck. The back, wings, and tail are ashen grey, washed with a perceptible tinge of blue, and the abdomen is reddish grey, as are the edges of the quill-feathers of the wing.

LONG-TAILED TITMOUSE.—*Parus caudátus*.

THE LONG-TAILED TITMOUSE is familiarly known throughout England, and is designated under different titles, according to the locality in which it resides, some of its popular names being derived from its shape, and others from its crest. In some parts of the country it is called "Long Tom," while in others it goes by the name of "Bottle-crested Tit."

This pretty little bird is a notable frequenter of trees, hedge-rows, and orchards, and is remarkable for its sociable habits, being generally seen in little troops of six or eight in number. It appears that the young birds always remain with their parents throughout the whole of the first year, so that when the brood happens to be a large one, as many as sixteen Long-tailed Titmice may be seen hopping and skipping about together. The troop is always under the command of one bird, probably one of the parents, who takes the lead, and is copied by the others, so that they seem to be playing at a constant game of "Follow my leader." The leader has a peculiar chirruping cry, which is easily recognisable, and which is always uttered as it flits from one branch to another. The nest of this species is undoubtedly the most wonderful example of bird architecture that is to be found in the British Islands, and is not exceeded in beauty by the home of any bird whatever. In form it somewhat resembles an egg, and it is built of moss, hair, a very little wool, the cocoon webs of spiders, and the silken hammocks of certain caterpillars, all woven into each other in the most admirable manner.

GROUP OF BRITISH WAGTAILS.

The PIED WAGTAIL (*Motacilla Yarrellii*) remains in England throughout the year, but generally retires to the southern counties during the winter, as it would otherwise be unable to obtain its food. Sometimes, however, where the springs are so copious that the water never entirely freezes, the Wagtail may be seen haunting its accustomed spot, and drawing a subsistence from the unfrozen waters. The more northern coasts are a favourite resort of the Wagtails, which run briskly along the edge of the advancing or receding tide, picking up any stray provender that may come within their reach.

The song of the Pied Wagtail is soft, low, and sweet, and is generally uttered in the early morning from the elevation of some lofty spot, such as the summit of a pointed rock, the roof of an outhouse, or the top of a paling. The bird is bold and familiar, coming quite close to human beings without displaying any fear, and even following the ploughman for the purpose of picking up the grubs and insects that are turned out of the soil by the share.

The nest of the Wagtail is generally placed at no great distance from the water, and is always built in some retired situation. Holes in walls, the hollows of aged trees, or niches in old gravel-pits are favourite localities with this bird. Heaps of large stones are also in great favour with the Wagtail, and I have generally found that whenever a pile of rough stones has remained for some time in the vicinity of water, a Wagtail's nest is almost invariably somewhere within it. I have also found the nest in heaps of dry brushwood piled up for the purpose of being cut into faggots. In every case the nest is placed at a considerable depth, and no small amount of care and ingenuity is needed to extract the eggs without damaging them. The eggs are generally four or five in number, and their colour is grey-white speckled with a great number of very small brown spots.

The YELLOW WAGTAIL, or RAY'S WAGTAIL, (*Motacilla sulphurea*) as it is sometimes termed, is very common in this country, and is partial to pasture land, where it revels among the insects that are roused by the tread of cattle.

It is not so fond of water as the pied species, and may often be met with upon the driest lands, far from any stream, busily employed in catching the beetles, flies, and other sun-loving insects. Even upon roads it may frequently be observed, tripping about with great celerity, and ever and anon picking up an insect, and celebrating its success by a wag of the tail. The name of Yellow Wagtail has been given to it on account of the light yellow hue which tinges the head and the entire under surface of the body. As, however, the preceding species also possesses a considerable amount of yellow in its colouring, the name of Ray's Wagtail has been given to this bird in honour of the illustrious naturalist.

It is generally seen in little flocks or troops. The colour of this bird is olive above, and light yellow beneath.

There are seven other English species, all much alike in their habits.

MEADOW PIPIT.—*Anthus pratensis.*

There are several kinds of Pipits in England, where they are often known by the name of Titlarks, because the spotted breasts and long claws of the hind toes resemble the same parts in the skylark.

In some places the Meadow-Pipit is called the Moss-cheeper, or Longtoe. Its colour is olive-brown above, and whitish below, with a few spots on the breast.

The Meadow Pipit may be seen throughout the year upon moors, waste lands, and marshy ground, changing its locality according to the season of the year. It is a pretty though rather sombre little bird, and is quick and active in its movements, often jerking its long tail in a fashion that reminds the observer of the wagtail's habits. It moves with considerable celerity, tripping over the rough and rocky ground which it frequents, and picking up insects with the stroke of its unerring beak. Its food, however, is of a mixed description, as in the crops of several individuals were found seeds, insects, and water-shells, some of the latter being entire.

The song of this bird is hardly deserving of the name, being rather a feeble and plaintive "cheeping" than a true song.

The Tree Pipit *(Anthus arboreus)* is able to perch on branches, its hind claws being shorter than those of the Meadow Pipit. It runs well and easily, and trips over rough ground with singular ease.

The song of this bird is sweeter and more powerful than that of the preceding species, and is generally given in a very curious manner. Taking advantage of some convenient tree, it hops from branch to branch, chirping merrily with each hop, and, after reaching the summit of the tree, perches for a few moments, and then launches itself into the air, for the purpose of continuing its ascent. Having accomplished this feat, the bird bursts into a triumphant strain of music, and, fluttering downwards as it sings, alights upon the same tree from which it had started, and, by successive leaps, again reaches the ground.

It is known from the Meadow Pipit by its larger size, flatter head, and shorter hind claws.

GIANT BREVE.—*Pitta Gigas.*

THE great family of the THRUSHES has many well known examples in England. Some of the foreign species are very curious. The Ant-Thrushes being, perhaps, among the most remarkable. These birds derive their name from their ant-eating propensities; and, contrary to the general rule among the Thrushes, their plumage is decorated with the most brilliant hues; some species being like living rainbows, and others glowing with scarlet, azure, and purple. They all have great round heads, thick bodies, strong beaks, and short legs.

The great ANT-THRUSH, which is also called the GIANT PITTA, or the GIANT BREVE, in allusion to its large dimensions, is a native of Surinam, and on account of its bright plumage, its quaint and peculiar shape, its very large head, very long legs, and peculiarly short wren-like tail, which looks exactly as if it had been neatly cropped, is one of the most singular birds of that prolific locality. In size it equals an English rook, but hardly looks so large as that well-known bird, on account of the short tail, which is entirely covered by the wings when they are closed. The general colour of this brilliant bird is a light cobalt blue, which extends over the whole of the back and tail, but is not quite so lustrous upon the wings. The quill-feathers of the wings are black, tipped with sky-blue, and the head, the surface of the neck, together with a stripe that runs partly round them, are black, and the bird is brownish grey below.

DIPPER.—*Hydróbates cinclus.*

The Ant Thrushes find an English representative in the well-known Dipper, or Water-Ousel, of our river-banks.

Without brilliant plumage or graceful shape, it is yet one of the most interesting of British birds, when watched in its favourite haunts. It always frequents rapid streams and channels, and, being a very shy and retiring bird, prefers those spots where the banks overhang the water, and are clothed with brushwood. Should the bed of the stream be broken up with rocks or large stones, and the fall be sufficiently sharp to wear away an occasional pool, the Dipper is all the better pleased with its home, and in such a locality may generally be found by a patient observer.

All the movements of this little bird are quick, jerking, and wren-like, and it is continually flirting its apology for a tail. Caring nothing for the frost of winter, so long as the water remains free from ice, the Dipper may be seen throughout the winter months, flitting from stone to stone with the most animated gestures, occasionally stopping to pick up some morsel of food, and ever and anon taking to the water, where it sometimes dives entirely out of sight, and at others merely walks into the shallows, and there flaps about with great rapidity.

The food of the Dipper seems to be exclusively of an animal character, and, in the various specimens which have been examined, consists of insects, small crustaceæ, and the spawn and fry of various fishes.

MOCKING BIRD.—*Mimus polyglottus.*

THE celebrated MOCKING BIRD of America belongs to the Thrush family.

This wonderful bird is not only a most admirable songster, but is capable of imitating almost every possible sound that meets its ear. It mocks all the birds of the forest, and decoys them around it by imitating their different voices, and if it comes near human habitations, it gains a great addition to its former stock of sounds, and lays up in its memory the various noises that are produced by man and his surroundings; introducing among its other imitations the barking of dogs, the harsh " setting " of saws, the whirring buzz of the millstone, the everlasting clack of the hoppers, the dull heavy blow of the mallet, and the cracking of splitting timbers, the fragments of songs whistled by the labourers, the creaking of ungreased wheels, the neighing of horses, the plaintive baa of the sheep, and the deep lowing of the oxen, together with all the innumerable and accidental sounds which are necessarily produced through human means. Unfortunately, the bird is rather apt to spoil his own wonderful song by a sudden introduction of one of these inharmonious sounds, so that the listener, whose ear is being delighted with a succession of the softest and richest-toned vocalists, will suddenly be electrified with the loud shriek of the angry hawk or the grating whirr of the grindstone.

MISSEL THRUSH.—*Turdus viscivorus*.

THE MISSEL THRUSH is one of the largest and handsomest of the species.

It is one of our resident birds, and on account of its great size, its combative nature, its brightly feathered breast, its rich voice, and sociable habits, is one of the best known of the British birds. About the beginning of April the Missel Thrush sets about its nest, and in general builds a large, weighty edifice, that can be seen through the leafless bushes from a great distance. Sometimes, however, the nest is concealed with the greatest care, and I cannot but think that in the latter case it is the work of some old bird, who has learnt caution through bitter experience.

The materials of which the nest is composed are the most varied that can be imagined. Every substance that can be woven into a nest is pressed into the service. Moss, hay, straw, dead leaves, and grasses, are among the ruling substances that are employed for the purpose, and the bird often adds manufactured products, such as scraps of rag, paper, string, or shavings.

FIELDFARE.—*Turdus pilaris.*

ANOTHER large example of the British Thrushes is found in the FIELDFARE.

This bird is one of the migratory species, making only a winter visit to this country, and often meeting a very inhospitable reception from the gun of the winter sportsboy. Very seldom is it seen in this country till November, and is often absent until the cold month of December, when it makes its appearance in great flocks, searching eagerly for food over the fields. At this period of the year they are very wild, and can with difficulty be approached within gunshot, as I have often experienced in my younger days.

RING OUSEL.—*Turdus torquátus.*

THE RING OUSEL is another British bird, and derives its name from the ring or band of white that partly surrounds the lower portion of the neck.

It is a shy and wary bird, shunning cultivated grounds and the human habitations, and withdrawing itself into the wildest and most hilly districts. It is a quick-flying, lively and active bird, and is said to afford fine sport to the falconer, owing to its singular adroitness and ingenuity in escaping the stroke of the hawk. It will quietly suffer the bird of prey to approach quite closely, screaming a defiance to the enemy and flitting quietly along a stone wall or rocky ground. Suddenly the hawk makes its swoop, and the Ring Ouzel disappears, having whisked into some hole in the stone, squeezed itself into a convenient crevice, or slipped over the other side of the wall just as the hawk shot past the spot on which it had been sitting.

The song of this bird is loud, clear, and sonorous, but contains a very few notes.

BLACKBIRD.—*Turdus merula*.

The common Blackbird is one of the best known of our native songsters. It sings beautifully; and its notes are very full and rich in their tone.

The nest of this bird is made very early in the spring, and is always carefully placed in the centre of some thick bush, a spreading holly-tree being a very favourite locality. It is a large, rough, but carefully constructed habitation, being made externally of grass, stems, and roots, plastered on the interior with a rather thick lining of coarse mud, which, when thoroughly dried, forms a kind of rude earthenware cup. A lining of fine grass is placed within the earthen cup, and, upon this lining, the five eggs are laid. These eggs are of a light greyish-blue ground-colour, splashed, spotted, and freckled over their entire surface with brown of various shades and intensity. The colouring of these eggs is extremely variable, even those of a single nest being very different in their appearance; and I once took a Blackbird's nest, in which the eggs were so curiously marked, that no one could have decided whether they belonged to a blackbird or a thrush. Sometimes the spots are almost wholly absent, and at other times the eggs are so covered with reddish-brown markings that the ground-colour is hardly discernible.

The colour of the full-grown male Blackbird is rich shining black, and his beak is orange. The female is brown.

SONG-THRUSH.—*Turdus músicus.*

The well-known Song-Thrush, or Throstle, as it is sometimes called, bears a deservedly high rank among our British birds of song.

The food of the Thrush is mostly of an animal character, and consists largely of worms, snails, slugs, and similar creatures. In eating snails it is very dexterous, taking them in its bill, battering them against a stone, until the shells are entirely crushed, and then swallowing the inclosed mollusc. When a Thrush has found a stone that suits his purpose peculiarly well, he brings all his snails to the spot, and leaves quite a large heap of empty snail-shells under the stone. One of the best examples that I have ever seen, was a large square boulder-stone, forming part of a rustic stile in Wiltshire. There was a large pile of shells immediately under the stone, and the ground was strewed for some distance with the crushed fragments that had evidently been trodden upon and carried away by the feet of passengers.

The Thrush does not, however, confine itself wholly to this kind of diet, but, in the autumn months, feeds largely on berries and different fruits, being very fond of cherries, and sometimes doing some damage to the orchards.

Sometimes the bird employs rather strange materials for its nest; and I know of an instance where a Thrush carried off a lace cap that was hanging on a clothes-line, and worked it into the sides of its nest.

SPOTTED GROUND THRUSH.—*Cinclosóma punctátus.*

AUSTRALIA possesses a curious and valued specimen of this group, which is popularly called the SPOTTED GROUND THRUSH, or GROUND DOVE.

This bird is found throughout the greater part of Australia and Van Diemen's Land, and on account of the delicacy of its flesh it is greatly prized by both natives and colonists. Being always attracted by certain localities, it may be easily found by every one who is acquainted with its habits. Unlike the generality of birds, it cares little for trees or bushes, and seldom is known to perch upon the branches, preferring the tops of low stone-covered hills, or rude and rocky gullies, having a decided preference for those which are clothed with grass and scrubby brushwood. The spaces between fallen trees are a favourite haunt of this bird.

The Spotted Ground Thrush is no great flyer, taking to wing with much reluctance, and seldom voluntarily raising itself in the air, except to fly from one side of a gully to another. When it does take to flight, especially if alarmed, it rises with a loud fluttering noise, and proceeds through the air in an irregular and dipping manner. To compensate however, for its imperfect power of wing, its legs are well developed, and render it an exceeding fast runner, so that it is able to conceal itself with great rapidity as soon as it finds cause of alarm.

The nest of this species is a very loose and negligent kind of structure, made of leaves, the inner bark of trees, and various vegetable substances, laid carelessly together in some casual depression in the ground.

GOLDEN ORIOLE.—*Oriölus gálbula.*

THE GOLDEN ORIOLE is sometimes, but rarely, seen in England. It derives its name from the golden yellow of its body, which contrasts so well with the jet black of its wings.

In Italy, this bird is quite common, and by the peasantry is supposed to announce the ripening of the fig, its peculiar cry being translated into a choice Italian sentence, signifying that the fruits have attained maturity. It is rather gregarious in its habits, generally associating in little flocks, and frequenting lofty trees and orchards, where it can obtain abundance of food.

It is an exceedingly shy bird, keeping carefully from man and his home, and only venturing into cultivated grounds for the sake of obtaining food. Even in such cases it is extremely cautious in its behaviour, and as it always takes the trouble to set sentries on guard, it cannot be approached without the greatest patience and wariness on the part of the sportsman or observer. Being generally found in the loneliest spots, and especially preferring the outskirts of forests, whence it can at once dive into the thick foliage and escape from danger, it often baffles the skill even of the practised fowler, who is forced to trust to the careful imitation of its note for his hope of getting within shot of this cunning bird. Moreover, the imitation must be exceedingly exact, for the ear of the Golden Oriole is wonderfully true and delicate.

KING BIRD.—*Tyrannus intrepidus.*

The family of the Flycatchers is a rather small, but interesting one.

The well-known King Bird of America is a good example of the tyrant Flycatchers, on account of their bold and combative habits. It fights every bird that dares to come near its nest; and although it is only eight inches long, it will attack an eagle without the least fear. Wilson writes the following remarks on this bird and its mode of fighting:—

"Hawks and crows, the bald eagle and the great black eagle, all equally dread *rencontre* with this dauntless little champion, who, as soon as he perceives one these last approaching, launches into the air to meet him, mounts to a considerable height above him, and darts down upon his back, sometimes fixing there, to the great annoyance of his sovereign, who, if no convenient retreat or resting-place be near, endeavours by various evolutions to rid himself of his merciless adversary.

"There is one bird, however, which, by its superior rapidity of flight, is sometimes more than a match for him; and I have several times witnessed his precipitous retreat before this active antagonist. This is the purple martin, one whose food and disposition is pretty similar to his own, but who has greatly the advantage of him on the wing, in eluding all his attacks, and teasing him as he pleases. I have also seen the red-hooded woodpecker, while clinging on a rail of the fence, amuse himself with the violence of the King Bird, and play *bo-peep* with him round the rail, while the latter, highly irritated, made every attempt, as he swept from side to side, to strike him, but in vain. All this turbulence, however, vanishes, as soon as his young are able to shift for themselves, and he is then as mild and peaceable as any other bird."

WHITE-SHAFTED FAN-TAIL.

Rhipidura Albíscapa.

THE WHITE-SHAFTED FANTAIL is a native of Australia, and is remarkable for the singular form of its nest. It is termed the Fantail on account of the manner in which it spreads the feathers of the tail while flying.

In its habits it is brisk, cheerful, and lively, mounting high into the air with a few rapid strokes of the wings, and then descending, upon some convenient bank in a headlong, reckless style, after turning completely over in the air after the fashion of the tumbler pigeons. While descending, it spreads its wings and tail widely, the latter organ being so broad as to resemble a feather fan. It is daring and confiding in its nature, permitting the close approach of human beings, haunting the neighbourhood of human habitations, and even boldly entering houses in chase of flies and other insects. Its song is not powerful or varied, but is full and pleasing, consisting of a soft and sweet twittering sound.

During the breeding season it becomes suddenly shy, wary, and restless, and should it perceive an enemy in too close proximity to its nest, puts in practice a series of rather transparent wiles in order to induce the intruder on its domestic joys to leave the vicinity. For this purpose it feigns lameness, and flutters before the supposed foe in a manner that is intended to induce a belief in its easy capture, and to lure it from the cherished spot where all its loves and hopes are concentrated.

The Pied and Spotted Flycatchers are common in England.

The Spotted Flycatcher is by far the more common of the two species, and has received several local names in allusion to its habits; the titles of Wall Bird and Beam Bird being those by which it is most frequently designated. It is one of the migrating birds, arriving in this country at a rather late season, being seldom seen before the middle or even the end of May. The reason for its late arrival is probably that, if the bird were to make an earlier appearance, the flying insects on which it feeds would not be hatched in sufficient numbers to ensure a proper supply of food for itself and young. It is a common bird throughout the whole of England and Ireland, and is also seen but not so frequently, in Scotland. It has a wide range of locality, having been observed in different parts of Europe, and extending its flight to Southern Africa.

This bird is fond of haunting parks, gardens, meadows, and shrubberies, always choosing those spots where flies are most common, and attaching itself to the same perch for many days in succession. When the Flycatcher inhabits any place where it has been accustomed to live undisturbed, it is a remarkably trustful bird.

The Pied Flycatcher is not so common as the Spotted species, and may be known by the pied black and white of its plumage.

PIED FLYCATCHER.
Muscicapa atricapilla.
SPOTTED FLYCATCHER.
Muscicapa grisola.

KING TODY.—*Muscivora régia.*

The last of the Flycatchers which we shall notice in this book is the singular and beautiful bird known by the name of King Tody, or Royal Great Crest, it is a native of Brazil, and may challenge competition with many of the flycatchers for elegance of form and beauty of colouring.

It is a very rare bird, being seldom brought to England, and to all appearance but little known in its native land. This species is chiefly remarkable for its splendid crest, which is capable of being lowered upon the neck, or raised almost perpendicularly, in which latter position it assumes a spreading and rounded form, like an open fan.

The feathers of the crest are long and slender, and spoon-shaped at their extremities. Each feather is bright chestnut-red for the greater part of its length, a narrow stripe of rich orange succeeds, and the tip is velvet black, encircled by a band of steel-blue. As may be supposed, the effect of its spread crest is remarkably fine and striking.

The upper parts of the body are dark chestnut-brown, rather deeper on the quill feathers of the wings. The throat, chest, and abdomen are pale fawn, warming towards chestnut on the central line. The total length of this bird is six inches and a half.

COCK OF THE ROCK.—*Rupícola aurantia*.

The family of the Chatterers now comes before our notice; the Manakins head the list. The largest and handsomest species of Manakin is the Cock of the Rock.

It is a native of Southern America and Guinea, and, as it is a solitary and extremely retiring bird, is but seldom seen except by those who go in special search of it. This bird is remarkable, not only for the bright orange-coloured plumage with which its whole body is covered, but for its beautiful crest, which extends over the head like the plume of an ancient helmet. It generally frequents the banks of rocky streams and deep sombre ravines, where it traverses the ground with much rapidity, by means of its powerful and well-developed legs. As it is a solitary and very wary bird, it is seldom shot by white men, the greater number of existing specimens having been procured by means of the poisoned arrow thrown through the deadly sumpitan, or blow-pipe, of the Macoushi Indians.

BELL BIRD, OR CAMPANERO.—*Arapunga alba.*

The most curious of this family is certainly the noisy little Bell Bird of Southern America.

The Bell Bird is about the size of an ordinary pigeon, and its plumage is quite white. From a pigeon it can easily be distinguished, even at some distance, by the curious horn-like structure which grows from its forehead, and rises to a height of some three inches when the bird is excited. This "horn" is jetty-black in colour, sprinkled very sparingly with little tufts of snowy-white down, and as it has a communication with the palate, has probably something to do with the bell-like sound of the voice.

WOOD SWALLOW.—*Artamus Sórdidus*.

The Wood Swallows, as they are termed, are found in many parts of the globe.

The common Wood Swallow, or Sordid Thrush, is common in Australia.

This Wood Swallow is remarkable for a habit which is perhaps unique among birds, and hitherto has only been observed in certain insects. A large flock of these birds will settle upon the branches of a tree, and gather together in a large cluster, precisely like bees when they swarm. Four or five birds suspend themselves to the under side of the bough, others come and cling to them, and in a short time the whole flock is hanging to the bough like a large swarm of bees. Mr. Gilbert, who first noticed this curious habit, states that he has seen the swarms as large as an ordinary bushel measure.

The nest of the Wood Swallow is cup-shaped and rather shallow, and is made of very slender twigs bound and lined with delicate fibrous roots. The locality in which the nest is placed is extremely variable, the bird seeming to be wonderfully capricious in its choice of a fit spot whereon to fix its residence. Sometimes it is placed in a low forked branch, at another time it will be buried in thick massy foliage, while it is sometimes found fixed against the trunk of a tree, resting on some protuberance of the bark, or lodged within some suitable cavity. The eggs are about four in number, are greyish-white, speckled and mottled very variably with grey and white.

GREAT DICRURUS.—*Dicrúrus grandis.*

The Wood Swallows, together with many other birds, are classed together under the name of Dicrurine, or Double-tailed Birds, because their tails are very deeply cleft. The most conspicuous of these birds is the remarkable and beautiful creature represented in the engraving. In its general outline this beautiful bird bears some analogy to the Leona nightjar, having two long feathery appendages, naked throughout the greater portion of their length and webbed only at their extremity. There is, however, this great difference, that in the Leona nightjar they proceed from the wings, whereas in the Great Dicrurus they are merely prolongations of the external tail-feathers. The colour of this bird is deep blue-black, like that of the raven, and its weird-like aspect is further strengthened by a large and well-developed crest that starts from the top of the head and bends backwards over the neck. A few of its feathers project slightly forwards so as to come beyond the base of the beak.

GREAT GREY SHRIKE.—*Lanius excubitor.*

We now arrive at the family of Shrikes, or Butcher Birds, whose character is given in the names by which they are distinguished. These birds are found in all parts of the globe, and in all countries are celebrated for their savage character. They are quite as rapacious as any of the hawk tribe, and in proportion to their size are much more destructive and bloodthirsty. They feed upon small mammalia, and birds of various kinds, especially preferring them while young and still unfledged, and upon several kinds of reptiles, and also find great part of their subsistence among the members of the insect world.

Of the true Shrikes we find an excellent example in the well-known Great Grey Shrike, a bird which is very common in many parts of Europe, especially in the more southern and warmer regions, but is generally scarce in England, visiting us, whenever it does make its appearance, in the winter season.

This bird eats mice, shrews, small or young birds, frogs, lizards, beetles, grass-hoppers, and many other creatures.

VIGOR'S BUSH SHRIKE.—*Thamnóphilus Vigorsii*.

THE BUSH SHRIKES are well represented by the beautiful VIGOR'S BUSH SHRIKE.

This bird is a native of Southern America, and is generally found in forests and thick brushwood, where it passes its time in a constant search after the small mammalia, birds, reptiles, and insects, on which it feeds. It is a large and rather powerful bird, and as it possesses a strong and sharply hooked beak, it is a very formidable foe to any creature which it may attack. Its claws are also powerful, curved and very sharp, so that the bird is aided by its feet as well as by its beak in the demolition of its prey. In order to enable the bird to prey among the rank herbage and thick massy foliage of the localities in which it dwells, its legs are long in proportion to the size of its body, and the grasp of its feet very strong, so that it is able to perch upon a bough or on the ground, and raise its head to some height while surveying the locality with its piercing glance. The wings are rather short and rounded.

PIPING CROW.—*Gymnorhina tibicen.*

The large and important family of the Crows now comes before us.

The Piping Crow Shrike, sometimes called the Magpie by the colonists, on account of its magpie-like white and black plumage, is a native of New South Wales, and, towards the interior, is very plentiful.

This bird is found in almost every part of the country; preferring, however, the open localities to the wooded districts, especially if they are cleared by artificial means. For the Piping Crow Shrike is a wonderfully trustful bird, attaching itself instinctively to mankind, and haunting the vicinity of barns and farmyards. On the very slightest encouragement, the bird will take possession of a barn, garden, or plantation; and, with the exception of a favoured few, will not suffer any of his friends to intrude upon his property. The owner of the garden is well repaid for his hospitality, by the rich and varied song which the bird pours forth in the early morning and towards evening, as if in gratitude for the protection which has been afforded it.

JAY.—*Gárrulus Glándarius.*

The common Jay is plentiful in most parts of England.

The ordinary note of the Jay is a rather soft cry, but the bird is a most adroit imitator of various sounds, particularly those of a harsh character. It has one especial harsh scream, which is its note of alarm, and serves to set on the alert, not only its own kind, but every other bird that happens to be within hearing. The sportsman is often baffled in his endeavours to get a shot at his game by the mingled curiosity and timidity of the Jay, which cannot hear a strange rustling, or see an unaccustomed object, without sneaking silently up to inspect it, and is so terribly frightened at the sight of a man, a dog, and a gun, that it dashes off in alarm, uttering its loud "squawk," which indicates to every bird and beast that danger is abroad.

In captivity the Jay soon learns to talk, and, even when caged, displays its imitative powers with considerable success, mocking the bleating of sheep, the cackling of poultry, the grunting of pigs, and even the neighing of horses, with wonderful truth.

The Jay, like all the crow tribe, will eat animal or vegetable substances, and will plunder the hoards of small quadrupeds, or swallow the owner with perfect impartiality. Young birds are a favourite food of the Jay, which is wonderfully clever at discovering nests and devouring the fledglings. Occasionally it even feeds upon birds, and has been seen to catch a full-grown thrush. Eggs, also, are great dainties with this bird, particularly those of pheasants and partridges, so that it is ranked among the "vermin" by all gamekeepers or owners of preserves.

BLUE JAY.—*Cyanócorax cristátus.*

THE BLUE JAY, so called from its colour, is an American bird.

The Blue Jay attacks owls whenever it meets with them, and never can see a hawk without giving the alarm, and rushing to the attack, backed up by other Jays, who never fail to offer their assistance to their comrade. Often they will assemble in some numbers, and buffet the unfortunate hawk with such relentless perseverance that they fairly drive him out of the neighbourhood; but sometimes the tables are reversed, and the hawk, turning suddenly on his persecutors, snaps up the foremost and boldest, and silently sails away into the thickest covert, bearing his screaming prey in his talons.

HUNTING CISSA.—*Cissa Sinensis.*

WHEN in full plumage, living, and in good condition, the HUNTING CISSA is certainly the most lovely of all the Crow tribe, but unfortunately the tints of its feathers are so exceedingly delicate, that they fade by the action of light even while the bird is living, and after its death are comparatively dull. Only for a day or two after moulting does the Hunting Cissa show itself in its true colours.

It is a brisk and lively bird, and like many others of the same group, is much given to imitating other birds, performing its mimicry with wonderful truth, and copying not only their voices, but even their peculiar gestures.

It is much more carnivorous in its tastes than would be imagined from an inspection of its form and plumage, and it possesses many of the habits of the shrikes, not only killing and eating the smaller birds, but hanging its food upon branches in true shrike fashion. It is an excellent hunter, and as it can be easily tamed and taught to hunt after small birds for the amusement of its owner, it has earned the name of Hunting Crow. In its native country it is very commonly kept in captivity, and even in England has lived for a considerable time in a cage in the gardens of the Zoological Society. The voice of the Hunting Cissa is loud and screeching.

The colour of this bird is bright grass-green, taking a yellowish tinge on the under parts of the body: Its wing is chestnut, mottled with black and white, and the tail is green, black, and white.

WANDERING PIE.

Temnúrus vagabundus.

THERE is one very curious and beautiful member of the Crow tribe, which lives in America, but is often killed, and the skin brought over to this country, on account of its elegant shape, and the bold, though not brilliant colours of its plumage.

This bird is a native of the Himalayas, and is found in some numbers spread over a large part of India. It is called the WANDERING PIE on account of its habit of wandering over a very large extent of country, travelling from place to place and finding its food as it best may, after the fashion of a begging friar.

This custom is quite opposed to the general habits of the Pies, who re remarkable for their attachment to definite localities, and can generally be found wherever the observer has discovered the particular spot which they have selected for their home. Mr. Gould thinks that its wandering habit may be occasioned by the necessity for obtaining subsistence, the Wandering Pie feeding more exclusively on fruits and other vegetables than is generally the case with the Crow tribe, and being therefore forced to range over a large extent of land in search of its food. Indeed, the short legs and very long tail of this species would quite unfit it for seeking its living on the ground, and clearly point out its arboreal habits.

The shape of this species is very remarkable, on account of the greatly elongated and elegantly shaped tail.

RAVEN.—*Corvus corax.*

THE RAVEN is a British bird, once common, but now seldom seen except in wild and uncultivated districts.

This truly handsome bird is spread over almost all portions of the globe, finding a livelihood wherever there are wide expanses of uncultivated ground, and only being driven from its home by the advance of cultivation and the consequent inhabitance of the soil by human beings. It is a solitary bird, living in the wildest district that it can find, and especially preferring those that are intersected with hills. In such places the Raven reigns supreme, hardly the eagle himself daring to contest the supremacy with so powerful, crafty, and strong-beaked a bird.

The food of the Raven is almost entirely of an animal nature, and there are few living things which the Raven will not eat whenever it finds an opportunity of so doing. Worms, grubs, caterpillars, and insects of all kinds are swallowed by hundreds, but the diet in which the Raven most delights is dead carrion. In consequence of this taste, the Raven may be found rather plentifully on the Scottish sheep-feeding grounds, where the flocks are of such immense size that the bird is sure to find a sufficiency of food among the daily dead; for its wings are large and powerful, and its daily range of flight is so great, that many thousands of sheep pass daily under its view, and it is tolerably sure in the day to find at least one dead sheep or lamb.

CROW.—*Corvus coróne.*

THE common CARRION CROW, so plentiful in this country, much resembles in habits and appearance, the bird which has just been described, and may almost be reckoned as a miniature raven.

In many of its customs the Crow is very raven-like, especially in its love for carrion, and its propensity for attacking the eyes of any dead or dying animal. Like the raven, it has been known to attack game of various kinds, although its inferior size forces it to call to its assistance the aid of one or more of its fellows, before it can successfully cope with the larger creatures. Rabbits and hares are frequently the prey of this bird, which pounces on them as they steal abroad to feed, and, while they are young, is able to kill and carry them off without difficulty.

The Crow also eats reptiles of various sorts, frogs and lizards being common dainties, and is a confirmed robber of other birds' nests; even carrying away the eggs of game and poultry, by the simple device of driving the beak through them and flying away with them. Even the large egg of the duck has thus been stolen by the Crow. Sometimes it goes to feed on the seashore, and there finds plenty of food among the crabs, shrimps, and shells that are found near low-water mark, and ingeniously cracks the harder shelled creatures, by flying with them to a great height, and letting them fall upon a convenient rock.

ROOK.—*Corvus frugilegus.*

The Rook is, perhaps, the best known among the British members of the Crow tribe. It may be known, even on the wing, from the common Crow, by the naked white skin about the eyes.

This bird feeds mostly on insects, grubs, and worms, and is very useful in killing these destructive creatures. It is very fond of the grub of the cockchaffer, a great fat, whitish creature, which lives under the ground, and eats the roots of grasses and other plants. It also eats multitudes of the wire-worms, which, if allowed to increase, without some such check, would destroy many a fine crop of wheat.

The Rook also feeds upon berries and various fruits, being especially fond of acorns, and having a curious habit of burying them in the earth before eating them, by which means, no doubt, many a noble oak-tree is planted. It also eats walnuts, and is fond of driving its bill into them, and so taking them from the tree. The cones of the Scotch fir are also favourite food with the Rook, which seizes them in its beak, and tries to pull them from the bough by main force; but if it should fail in this attempt, it drags the bough downwards, and then lets it spring up with a sudden jerk, so as to shake off the cones.

Some farmers think that the Rook does harm to their fields, by eating the seed and young corn, and kill it whenever they are able.

JACKDAW.—*Corvus monédula.*

THE smallest of the British Crows is the well known JACKDAW, a bird of great wit and humour, and one that has an extraordinary attachment to man and his habitations.

Although of similar form, and black of plumage, the Jackdaw may easily be distinguished from either the rook or the crow by the grey patch upon the crown of the head and back of the neck, which is very conspicuous, and can be seen at a considerable distance. The voice, too, is entirely different from the caw of the rook, or the hoarse cry of the crow, and as the bird is very talkative, it soon announces itself by the tone of its voice. It generally takes up its home near houses, and is fond of nesting in old buildings, especially preferring the steeples and towers of churches and similar edifices, where its nest and young are safe from the depredations of stoats, weasels, and other destroyers. Indeed, there are few places where Jackdaws will not build, provided that they are tolerably steep and high.

The nest of the Jackdaw is a very rude structure of sticks, lined, or rather covered, with hay, wool, feathers, and all kinds of substances of a warm kind for eggs and young. It is placed in various localities, generally in buildings or rocks, but has often been found in hollow trees, and even in the holes of rabbit-warrens, the last-mentioned spot being a very remarkable one, as the young birds must be in constant danger of marauding stoats and weasels.

GREAT-BILLED CROW.—*Corvus crassirostris.*

The remarkable bird which has very appropriately been called the Great-Billed Crow, is the most singular example of the whole tribe.

In its dimensions it is much larger than an ordinary crow, and rather smaller than a raven, for which bird it might be taken, but for the extraordinary beak. The bill of this species is so large as to remind the observer of a toucan or a puffin, and the bite of such a powerful weapon must be most formidable. It is very deep, thick and rounded, becoming wider at the top and deeply ridged, curving suddenly to a point, and very sharp at its extremity.

NUTCRACKER.—*Nucifraga caryocatactes.*

The small but handsome and striking bird which is popularly called the Nutcracker Crow, is extremely scarce in England, having but seldom been discovered upon the British Islands.

As it is so conspicuous a bird, it would not escape the notice of even the most careless observer, and we may be sure that it has very seldom, if ever, visited England without its arrival being noted. It is tolerably common in several parts of Europe, and has been seen in Switzerland in large flocks, feeding upon the seeds of the pine-trees after the fashion that has gained for the bird its name of Nutcracker. This species feeds mostly upon seeds, especially those of the pine, the beech, and various nuts, and it breaks the hard shells by fixing the nut or pine-cone in a convenient crevice, and hammering with its beak until it has exposed the kernel. Indeed, while engaged in this pursuit, its movements are almost precisely those of the common nuthatch.

It does not, however, feed wholly on seeds, but varies its diet with insect food, in pursuit of which it ranges for a considerable distance over the country, seeking the insects either on the ground or on the trees—generally the latter.

By means of the powerful bill and neck muscles, the Nutcracker is able to dig out the large-bodied grubs which are found deeply buried in the wood of various trees, and which it discovers through its quick sense of sight and hearing.

MAGPIE.—*Pica caudáta.*

The Magpie is common in England, and is well-known on account of its beautiful pied plumage and its mischievous character. It mostly eats animal food, and is a terrible robber of nests, carrying off the eggs, and even dragging the young birds out of their home.

The nest of the Magpie is a rather complicated edifice, domed, with an entrance at the side, and mostly formed on the exterior of thorns, so as to afford an effectual protection against any foe who endeavours to force admittance into the fortress. Generally the nest is placed at the very summit of some lofty tree, the bird usually preferring those trees which run for many feet without a branch.

BALD FRUIT CROW.—*Gymnocéphalus calvus.*

The Bald Fruit Crow is one of a little group of birds which are found in South America.

This species is equal to the English Crow in size, and is altogether of a thicker and larger make. It is very common in Guinea. The head of the Bald Fruit Crow is very large and heavily made, and the whole front of the bird is totally bare, like that of the leatherhead, already described and figured. Many naturalists think that while the Bald Fruit Crow is still young, its head is clothed with feathers, together with the remainder of the body, and that like the rook of Europe it loses the feathers when it attains maturity. There has been considerable argument on the subject, but it seems to have been tolerably well settled that the young bird is feathered and the old bird is bare.

It is seldom seen upon the ground, finding its food among the branches, and confining itself almost exclusively to their shelter.

UMBRELLA BIRD.—*Cephalópterus ornátus.*

The group of the Fruit Crows may lay claim to the credit of reckoning among their number one of the most singular of the feathered tribe. The Umbrella Bird is a truly remarkable creature, and from the extraordinary mode in which its plumage is arranged, never fails of attracting the attention of the most indifferent spectator.

The bird is a native of the islands of the South American rivers—being seldom if ever seen on the main land—whence it is not unfrequently brought by collectors, as there is always a ready sale for its skin, either to serve as an ornament in glass cases, or a specimen for a museum. In dimensions the Umbrella Bird equals the common crow of England, and but for the curious plume which adorns its head, and the tuft which hangs from its breast, might be mistaken at a distance for that bird. The general colour of this species is rich shining black, glazed with varying tints of blue and purple, like the feathers of the magpie's tail.

The Chough is one of a little group of birds called the Scarlet Crows, on account of the red beak and legs possessed by some of them.

The Chough is a coast bird, loving rocks and stones, and having a great dislike to grass or hedges of every kind. When in search of food it will venture some little distance inland, and has been observed in the act of following the ploughman, after the manner of the rook, busily engaged in picking up the grubs that are unearthed. Sometimes it will feed upon berries and grain, but evidently prefers animal food, pecking its prey out of the crevices among the rocks with great rapidity and certainty of aim, its long and curved beak aiding it in drawing the concealed insects out of their hiding-places. Cornwall is the chief resting-place of the Chough, but it is also found in many other parts of England and the British Isles.

It can be easily tamed if taken when young, and is when domesticated as amusing a bird as the rest of its tribe. In the garden it is rather useful, as it devours numbers of insects, continually searching for them in the crevices of walls and under the bark of trees.

CHOUGH.—*Corácia Gracula.*

It seems to reject worms, but is very fond of the mischievous cockchaffers, eating the small summer chaffer whole, but pulling the common cockchaffer to pieces before eating it.

As is the case with nearly all coast birds, the Chough builds its nest at no great distance from the sea, generally choosing some convenient crevice in a cliff or an old ruin near the sea-shore.

EMERALD BIRD OF PARADISE.—*Paradisea Apoda.*   KING BIRD OF PARADISE.—*Paradisea Regia.*

EMERALD BIRD OF PARADISE, AND KING BIRD OF PARADISE.

The magnificent birds in this engraving, are called, from their exceeding beauty, the BIRDS OF PARADISE.

The upper figure, with the cataract of white plumes, is the EMERALD PARADISE BIRD, so called from the emerald green colour which decorates part of its plumage.

This most lovely bird is a native of New Guinea, where it is far from uncommon, and is annually killed in great numbers for the sake of its plumage, which always commands a high price in the market. It is a very retiring bird, concealing itself during the day in the thick foliage of the teak tree, and only coming from the green shelter at the rising and setting of the sun, for the purpose of obtaining food. Almost the only successful method of shooting the Emerald Paradise Bird is to visit a teak or fig-tree before dawn, take up a position under the branches, and there wait patiently until one of the birds comes to settle upon the branches, or leaves the spot which has sheltered it during the night.

This bird is rather tenacious of life, and unless killed instantly is sure to make its escape amid the dense brushwood that grows luxuriantly beneath the trees, and if the sportsman ventured to chase a wounded bird amid the bushes, he would, in all probability, lose his way and perish of hunger. Those sportsmen, therefore, who desire to shoot this bird always provide themselves with guns that will carry their charge to a great distance, and employ very large shot for the purpose, as the bird always perches on the summits of the loftiest trees of the neighbourhood, and would not be much damaged by the shot ordinarily used in shooting.

This species is very suspicious, so that the sportsman must maintain a profound silence, or not a bird will show itself or utter its loud full cry, by which the hunter's attention is directed to his victim.

The colour of this splendid bird is chocolate brown above, and flashing emerald green upon the forehead, throat, and chest. The wonderful floating plumes that rise from the flanks, and descend in such graceful curves, are white, with a golden tint. Only the full grown male has these beautiful plumes.

In the right hand corner and at the bottom of the engraving, is the KING BIRD OF PARADISE, so called because it was once supposed to reign over the other species. It is a very little bird, the body being scarcely larger than that of a common sparrow, and is remarkable for the way in which its plumage is arranged, as will be seen from an examination of the engraving.

The colour of this bird is chestnut above, and white below. The band across the chest is golden-green, the fan-like plume of the shoulders is brown tipped with green, and the long slender shafts of the tail are green at the tips.

GOLDEN BIRD OF PARADISE.—*Paradisea Sexsetacea.*

The Golden Bird of Paradise is a remarkable bird, on account of the curious feathers which spring from the head, three on each side, bare for the greater part of their length, and furnished with a little patch of web at their extremities. These curious shafts are movable, as the bird possesses the power of raising them so as to stand out on each side of the head, or permitting them to hang loosely down the sides of the neck. The flanks are decorated with massive plumes of a jetty black, that can also be raised or lowered at the pleasure of the bird, and fall over the wings and tail so as nearly to conceal them.

SPOTTED BOWER BIRD.—*Chlamydéra maculáta.*

We now come to the Starlings, headed by the curious Bower Birds, so called from the bowers, or playing-places, which they build.

These birds are natives of Australia, and are in the habit of building these bowers on the ground, mostly sheltered by some large tree. They are made of twigs, very cleverly arranged, and the birds amuse themselves by running through them, like children at play. At the entrance the bird collects all the light objects it can find, such as bones, shells, and parrots' feathers.

So persevering are these birds in carrying off anything that may strike their fancy, that they have been known to steal a stone tomahawk, some blue cotton rags, and an old tobacco-pipe. Two of these bowers are now in the nest-room of the British Museum, and at the Zoological Gardens the Bower Bird may be seen hard at work at its surface, fastening the twigs or adorning the entrances, and ever and anon running through the edifice with a curious loud full cry, that always attracts the attention of a passer-by.

Of the STARLINGS we have two well-known English examples. The first of these, the ROSE-COLOURED PASTOR, is a scarce bird in England, though occasionally seen in our islands.

Although of rare occurrence in England, these birds are very common in many other countries; and, in some parts of India, are so numerous that forty or fifty have been killed at a single shot, and they are said, by the agriculturists, to be hardly less destructive than locusts. Like the common Starling, the Rose-coloured Pastor always flies in flocks, and seems to possess many of the habits which belong to the beef-eaters, perching on the backs of cattle, and feeding on the parasitic insects and grubs which are generally found in such situations. On account of this habit of frequenting the cattle-field and the sheep-fold, the bird has received the title of Pastor, or shepherd. It feeds chiefly on insects; but, in the autumn months, varies its diet with ripe fruits.

ROSE-COLOURED PASTOR.

Pastor roséus.

The Rose-coloured Pastor possesses a rather flexible voice; its ordinary cry is rather harsh and grating, but the bird is able to modulate its voice, so as to imitate the tones of various other members of the feathered tribe.

The colour of this bird is glossy purple black upon the head, neck, wings, and tail, and rose-pink on the breast and back. Its head is decorated with a crest of long flowing feathers of a rich violet black. This beautiful plumage is not completed until the bird is three years old.

The Common Starling is one of the handsomest of our British birds, the bright mottlings of its plumage, the vivacity of its movements, and the elegance of its form, rendering it a truly beautiful bird.

It is very common in all parts of the British Isles, as well as in many other countries, and assembles in vast flocks of many thousands in number, enormous accessions being made to their ranks after the breeding season. These vast assemblies are seen to best advantage in the fenny districts, where they couch for the night amid the osiers and aquatic plants, and often crush whole acres to the ground by their united weight. In their flight the Starlings are most wonderful birds, each flock, no matter how large its dimensions, seeming to be under the command of one single bird, and to obey his voice with an instantaneous action which appears little short of a miracle. A whole cloud of Starlings may often be seen flying along at a considerable elevation from the ground, darkening the sky as they pass overhead, when of a sudden the flock becomes invisible, every bird having turned itself on its side, so as to present only the edge of its wings to the eye. The whole body will then separate into several divisions, each division wheeling with the most wonderful accuracy, and after again uniting their forces they resume their onward progress to the feeding-ground or resting-place.

The colour of the Starling is dark purple-green, spotted with white.

COMMON STARLING.—*Sturnus vulgaris.*

ORCHARD ORIOLE.—*Xanthornis varius.*

The Orchard Oriole is very common in many parts of America, and is very remarkable for the nest which it builds.

The nest of the Orchard Oriole is a truly wonderful structure, woven into a bag or purse-like shape from long grasses, almost as if it had been fashioned in a loom, and so firmly constructed that it will withstand no small amount of rough treatment before its texture gives way. In one of these purse-like nests now lying before me, I find that the bird often employs two and sometimes three threads simultaneously, and that several of these double threads pass over the branch to which the nest is hung, and are then carried to the very bottom of the purse, so as to support the structure in the firmest possible manner.

The entrance is from above, and near the mouth; the nest is comparatively slight in texture, becoming thicker and more compact near the foot, where the eggs and young are laid. The entrance of the nest is generally lined with some soft downy seeds. So admirably does the bird's beak weave this remarkable nest, that an old lady to whom Wilson exhibited one of these structures, remarked that the Orchard Oriole might be taught to darn stockings.

The size and form of the nest vary very greatly according to the climate in which the bird lives, and the kind of tree on which its home is placed.

The colour of this bird is black and brown, with a little white.

BALTIMORE ORIOLE.—*Yphantes Baltimore.*

The Baltimore Oriole is another of the hang-nest birds, and is common in North America.

The nest of the Baltimore Oriole is somewhat similar to that of the preceding species, although it is generally of a thicker and tougher substance, and more ingeniously woven. The materials of which this beautiful habitation is made are flax, various kinds of vegetable fibres, mud, and hair, matted together, so as to resemble felt in consistency.

RUFOUS-NECKED WEAVER BIRD.—*Hyphantornis textor.*

The Weaver Birds are natives of Africa and India, and are remarkable for building very singular nests, even more curious than those of the Orchard and Baltimore Orioles. There are many of these birds, all building their nests in different positions. The Sociable Weaver Bird, for instance, makes a nest like a great honey-comb, many hundred birds inhabiting the same cluster of nests, all of which are made under the shelter of one roof. The Mahali Weaver makes a nest like a grass bottle, all the ends of the stalks sticking out on every side.

The Rufous-necked Weaver is also an inhabitant of Africa, being found in Senegal, Congo, and other hot portions of that continent.

By many persons this species is known by the name of the Capmore Weaver, a term which is evidently nothing but a corruption of Buffon's name for the same bird, namely, " Le Cap-noir," or Blackcap Weaver. It is a brisk and lively bird, and possesses a cheerful though not very melodious song. It has often been brought to Europe, and is able to withstand the effects of confinement with some hardihood, living for several years in a cage. Some of these caged birds carried into captivity the habits of freedom; and, as soon as the spring made its welcome appearance, they gathered together every stem of grass or blade of hay, and, by interweaving these materials among the wires of their cage, did their utmost to construct a nest. The food of this bird consists mostly of the beetles and other hard-shelled insects; and, in order to enable it to crush their defensive armour, which is extremely strong in many of the African beetles, its beak is powerful, and its edges somewhat curved. Seeds of various kinds also form part of its diet; and the undulating edge of the bill is quite as useful in shelling the seeds as in crushing the insects.

HAWFINCH, OR GROSBEAK.—*Coccothraustes vulgaris.*

The Grosbeaks derive their name from their large and thick bills.

The common Grosbeak, or Hawfinch, is plentiful in England; but as it is a shy bird, is not often seen. So extremely wary is the Hawfinch, that to approach within gunshot is a very difficult matter, and can seldom be accomplished without the assistance of a call-bird, or by imitating the call-note, which bears some resemblance to that of a robin. It feeds chiefly on the various wild berries, not rejecting even the hard stones of plums and the laurel-berries. In the spring it is apt to make inroads in the early dawn upon the cultivated grounds, and has an especial liking for peas, among which it often works dire havoc.

It associates in flocks varying in number from ten to two hundred, and always being greatest after the breeding season. It remains in England throughout the year, Epping Forest being one of its chief strongholds, as it abounds in berries of various kinds, is within a reasonable distance of cultivated grounds, and affords an excellent retreat.

When in the forest, the bird generally perches upon the extreme top of some lofty tree, from whence it keeps so complete a watch that hardly a weasel could steal upon it without being perceived and its presence reported by an alarm note.

The nest of the Hawfinch is not remarkable either for elegance or peculiarity of form.

BLACK AND YELLOW GROSBEAK.

Coccothraustes melanoxanthus.

MANY species of Grosbeak are found in different parts of the world, some being of most beautiful colours, while others are comparatively plain. The Cardinal Grosbeak of America is light scarlet and black, and the BLACK AND YELLOW GROSBEAK is decorated with the colours from which it derives its name.

The habits of this bird are like those of the generality of Grosbeaks.

It is one of the Asiatic birds, and its ordinary habitation is in the northern parts of India; but it is a bird of strong wing, and often wanders as far as Central India in search of food. Like others of the same group, it mostly feeds on berries and various stone-fruits, crushing even the hard-shelled seeds and stones in its thick and powerful beak. Even at a distance, this bird is very conspicuous on account of the bold and dashing manner in which the whole of the plumage is variegated with black, white, and yellow, all these colours being of the purest and brightest quality.

The whole of the upper surface and the breast are deep jetty black, with a slight silken gloss when the bird is in good condition. A few snowy white spots appear on some of the feathers of the wing, and several of the primaries, together with the whole of the secondaries, are edged with the same hue, thus presenting a very strong contrast to the jetty feathers of the back. The female is easily distinguished from her mate, as the upper surface is dusky black, largely mottled with yellow upon the head, neck, and back.

SCARLET TANAGER.—*Pyranga rubra.*

The Scarlet Tanager of America, so called on account of the bright scarlet of the plumage, is a very handsome bird, the black wings and tail contrasting boldly with the bright hue of the body.

It is possessed of a tolerable, though not especially musical voice. This is one of the migratory species, arriving in the northern portions of the United States about the end of April, and remaining until the breeding season is over. The nest is made of rather rough materials, such as flax-stalks and dry grass, and is so loosely put together that the light is perceptible through the interstices of the walls. The number of eggs is generally three, and their colour is dullish blue, variegated with brown and purplish spots. While engaged in the business of incubation, both birds are extremely terrified at the presence of any strange object, and if a human being approaches the nest, the male flies to a little distance and keeps cautiously aloof, peering through the boughs at the foe, and constantly fearful of being seen. The female also leaves the nest, but continues to fly restlessly about her home, hovering over the eggs or young in great distress. When, however, the young are hatched, the male parent takes his full share in attending upon them, and cares nothing for being seen.

GROUP OF FINCHES.

CHAFFINCH.—*Fringilla cælebs.* GOLDFINCH.—*Fringilla carduélis.*

The Finches are all little birds, many and brightly coloured.

The Chaffinch is one of our commonest field birds, being spread over the whole of England in very great numbers, and frequenting hedges, fields, and gardens with equal impartiality. It is a most gay and lively little bird, and whether singly, or assembled in large flocks, it always adds much life to the landscape, and delights the eye of every one who is not a farmer or a gardener, both of which personages wage deadly war against the bright little bird. For the Chaffinch is apt at times to be a sad thief, and has a strong liking for young and tender vegetables.

Of all the British Finches, none is so truly handsome as the Goldfinch, a bird whose bright hues suffer but little even when it is placed in close proximity to the more gaudy Finches of tropical climates. There are few prettier sights than to watch a cloud of goldfinches fluttering along an hedge, chasing the thistledown as it is whirled away by the breeze, and uttering all the while their sweet merry notes.

GREENFINCH.—*Fringilla chloris.* LINNET.—*Fringilla cannábina.*

The Greenfinch is one of our commonest birds. It is mostly found in hedges, bushes, and copses, and as it is a bold and familiar bird, is in the habit of frequenting the habitations of men, and even building its nest within close proximity to houses or gardens.

Few birds are better known than the Linnet, although the change of plumage to which it is subject in the different seasons of the year has caused the same bird, while in its winter plumage, to be considered as distinct from the same individual in its summer dress.

CANARY.—*Carduélis canária*.

THE pretty little CANARY BIRD, so prized as a domestic pet, derives its name from the locality whence it was originally brought.

Rather more than three hundred years ago, a ship was partly laden with little green birds captured in the Canary Islands; and, having been wrecked near Elba, the birds made their escape, flew to the island, and there settled themselves. Numbers of them were caught by the inhabitants, and, on account of their sprightly vivacity and the brilliancy of their voice, they soon became great favourites, and rapidly spread over Europe.

The original colour of the Canary is not the bright yellow with which its feathers are usually tinted, but a kind of dappled olive green, black, and yellow, either colour predominating according to circumstances. By careful management, however, the bird-fanciers are able to procure Canaries of every tint between the three colours, and have instituted a set of rules by which the quality and arrangement of the colouring is reduced to a regular system. Still, the original dappled green is always apt to make its appearance; and even when two light-coloured birds are mated, a green young one is pretty sure to be found in the nest.

It is a lively little bird, delighting in company, and being very easily tamed. It is also docile and intelligent, and can be taught to perform many pretty tricks.

SPARROW.—*Passer domésticus.*

The Sparrow is remarkable for the manner in which it follows mankind, and attaches itself to houses and cities.

When in the country, the Sparrow feeds almost wholly on insects and grain, the former being procured in the spring and early summer, and the latter in autumn and winter. As these birds assemble in large flocks, and are always very plentiful, they devour great quantities of grain, and are consequently much persecuted by the farmer, and their numbers thinned by guns, traps, nets, and all kinds of devices. Yet their services in insect-killing are so great as to render them most useful birds to the agriculturist. A single pair of these birds have been watched during a whole day, and were seen to convey to their young no less than forty grubs per hour, making an average exceeding three thousand in the course of the week. In every case where the Sparrows have been extirpated, there has been a proportional decrease in the crops from the ravages of insects.

TREE SPARROW.—*Passer montánus.*

THE TREE SPARROW may readily be distinguished from the preceding species by the chestnut head, the triangular patch of black on the cheeks, and the browner white of the lower surface of the body.

This bird is not nearly so common as the house Sparrow, and generally places its nest in trees, in preference to thatch and walls. Sometimes, however, it follows the common Sparrow in the building of its domicile, and has been known to place its nest in the deserted home of a crow or rook, making a dome like that of the common Sparrow when building in trees. Occasionally it has been observed to build its nest in the hollow of a tree, and to take possession of a hole that had formerly been occupied by the woodpecker. The eggs are different in hue from those of the common Sparrow, being dullish white, covered entirely with very light dots of ashen brown. Their number is generally from four to six.

YELLOW-BUNTING, OR YELLOW-AMMER.—*Emberíza citrinella*.

The Buntings are known by their sharp conical bills, with the edges of the upper mandible rounded and slightly turned inwards, and the knob on the palate. They are common in most parts of the world, are sociable during the winter months, and, in some cases, become so fat upon the autumn grain, that they are considered great dainties.

One of the most familiar of all these birds is the Yellow-Bunting, or Yellow-Ammer, as it is often called.

This lively bird frequents our fields and hedgerows, and is remarkable for a curious mixture of wariness and curiosity, the latter feeling impelling it to observe a traveller with great attention, and the former to keep out of reach of any missile. So, in walking along a country lane, the passenger is often preceded by one or more of these birds, which always keeps about seventy or eighty yards in advance, and flutters in and out of the hedges or trees with a peculiar and unmistakeable flirt of the wings and tail.

In rustic parlance, a "rough gripe" is the place wherein to look for the Yellow-Ammer's nest. It is a neatly built edifice, composed chiefly of grasses, and lined with hair.

The colour of the Yellow-Ammer is bright yellow mottled with brown and black.

SKYLARK.—*Alauda arvensis.*

The Larks are known by the very long claw of the hind toe, and the great length of the "tertiary" quill feathers of the wings. A very common English species is the well-known Skylark.

This bird is very plentiful all over England, and may be seen throughout the spring and early summer months, fluttering high in the air, and warbling its light and lively song at a height that almost renders it invisible. In the autumn and winter, the Larks assemble in large flocks, and are killed in great numbers for the sake of their flesh, which is very delicate and well-flavoured.

BULLFINCH.—*Pyrrhular ubicilla.*

The well-known Bullfinch is, perhaps, rather more familiar as a cage bird than as a denizen of the wood, for it is so remarkably shy and retiring in its habits, that it keeps itself sedulously out of sight, and though bold enough in the pursuit of food, invading the orchards and gardens with considerable audacity, it yet has a careful eye to its own safety, and seldom comes within reach of gunshot.

It cares little for open country, preferring cultivated grounds, woods, and copses, and is very fond of orchards and fruit-gardens, finding there its greatest supply of food. This bird seems to feed almost wholly on buds during their season, and is consequently shot without mercy by the owners of fruit-gardens. The Bullfinch has a curious propensity for selecting those buds which would produce fruit, so that the leafage of the tree is not at all diminished. Although the general verdict of the garden-keeping public goes against the Bullfinch, there are, nevertheless, some owners of gardens who are willing to say a kind word for Bully, and who assert that its mischievous propensities have been much overrated.

It is a handsome little bird, its thick bullet head, chin, wings, and tail being jetty black, the sides of the face, the throat, and under parts light chestnut, and the back soft grey.

CROSSBILL.—*Loxia curvirostris*.

THE CROSSBILLS, of which three species are known to inhabit England, are most remarkable birds, and have long been celebrated on account of the singular form of beak from which they derive their name.

In all these birds, the two mandibles completely cross one another, so that at first sight the structure appears to prohibit the bird from picking up seeds or feeding itself in any way. But when the Crossbill is seen feeding, it speedily proves itself to be favoured with all the ordinary faculties of birds, and to be as capable of obtaining its food as any of the straight-beaked birds.

The food of the Crossbill consists almost, if not wholly, of seeds, which it obtains in a very curious manner. It is very fond of apple-pips; and, settling on the tree where ripe apples are to be found, attacks the fruit with its beak, and in a very few moments cuts a hole fairly into the "core," from which it picks out the seeds daintily and eats them, rejecting the ripe pulpy fruit in which they had been enveloped.

This bird is also very fond of the seeds of cone-bearing trees, and haunts the pine-forests in great numbers. While engaged in eating, it breaks the cones from branches, and, holding them firmly in its feet, after the fashion of the parrots, inserts its beak below the scales, wrenches them away, and with its bone-tipped tongue, scoops out the seed.

SENEGAL COLY.—*Colius macrocercus.*

The Colies are inhabitants of Africa and India; and as their plumage is of a soft and silken character, and generally of sober tints, they often go by the name of Mouse-birds, a title which is also due to their mouse-like manner of creeping among the boughs or trees.

The Senegal, or Long-tailed Coly, is found in Africa, in the country from which it derives its name.

It is a pretty bird, and, as it traverses the branches, has a peculiarly elegant appearance; its long tail seeming to balance it in the extraordinary and varied attitudes which it assumes, and its highly movable crest being continually raised or depressed, giving it a very spirited aspect.

It is a gregarious bird, living in little companies of four or five in number, and is continually jumping and running about the branches in search of its food, which consists of fruit and buds. The grasp of its feet is very powerful, as much so, indeed, as that of the parrot; and, while traversing the boughs, it may often be seen hanging by its feet, with its head downward, and occasionally remaining for sometime suspended by a single foot. In climbing from one branch to another, as in lowering themselves, the Colies frequently use their beaks to aid them, after the well-known practice of the parrots.

The colour of the Senegal Coly is greyish chestnut above, and pearl grey below.

WHITE-CRESTED TOURACO.—*Turacus Albocristatus.*

THE WHITE-CRESTED TOURACO belongs to the little group of birds called PLANTAIN-EATERS, from their mode of feeding.

This bird is remarkable not only for its handsome plumage, but for its peculiar customs. It is suspicious and wary, and has a peculiar talent for concealing itself. Let a White-crested Touraco only take the alarm, and in a second of time it will be so well hidden that even a practised eye can scarcely obtain a clue to its whereabouts.

It is generally to be found among the branches of trees, and if it should be alarmed, and fly from one tree to another, it will vanish from sight so rapidly that the only way to get a shot at it is by sending some one up the tree to beat each bough in succession.

Some of these birds are extremely inquisitive, and, in spite of their **native** caution, will follow a traveller for miles.

BLUE PLANTAIN-EATER.—*Schizorhis gigantea.*

The Blue Plantain-eater whose colour may be known by its popular title, is generally to be found on the lofty trees that skirt the edges of streams, either perched demurely on the boughs, or flitting rapidly through them in search of the fruits and insects on which it feeds.

It does not fly well, and seldom trusts itself to the air, except to pass from one tree to another.

The voice of this and other Plantain-eaters is always of a loud character.

HOATZIN.—*Opisthócomus cristatus.*

The very remarkable Hoatzin, or Crested Touraco, is a very fine bird, being nearly as large as a peacock, and having somewhat of the same sort of gait and mode of carriage.

This bird is a native of tropical America, being found in Guiana and the Brazils, where it assembles together in large flocks, on the banks of creeks and rivers. Its colour is brown above, striped with white, and the breast and throat are light brown washed with grey.

GROUP OF HORNBILLS.

There are many strange and wonderful forms among the feathered tribes; but there are, perhaps, none which more astonish the beholder who sees them for the first time, than the group of birds known by the name of HORNBILLS.

They are all distinguished by a very large beak, to which is added a singular helmet-like appendage, equalling the beak itself in some species, while in others it is so small as to attract but little notice. On account of the enormous size of the beak and the helmet, which in some species recede to the crown of the head, the bird appears to be overweighted by the mass of horny substance which it has to carry; but on a closer investigation, the whole structure is found to be singularly light, and yet very strong.

On cutting asunder the beak and helmet of a Hornbill, we find that the outer shell of horny substance is very thin indeed, scarcely thicker than the paper on which this description is printed, and that the whole interior is composed of numerous honey-combed cells, with very thin walls and very wide spaces, the walls of the cells being so arranged as to give every part strength when the bill is used for biting, and with a very slight expenditure of material. The general appearance of the dried head of a Hornbill, with its delicate cellular arrangements, and its thin polished bony shell, is not unlike the well-known shell of the paper nautilus, and crumbles in the grasp almost as easily.

Five species of Hornbills are shown in this engraving. The upper figure is the common RHINOCEROS HORNBILL (*Búceros Rhinóceros*); the handsome, but smaller bird on its left is the WHITE-CRESTED HORNBILL (*Búceros albocristátus*). Of the two figures that occupy the middle of the drawing, the left bird represents the CRESTED HORNBILL (*Búceros cristatus*), and that on the right is the TWO-HORNED HORNBILL (*Búceros bicornis*); the smaller bird at the bottom is the WOODPECKER HORNBILL (*Búceros Pica*).

In all the Hornbills, the beak varies greatly in proportion to the age of the individual, the helmet being almost imperceptible when it is first hatched, and the bill not very striking in its dimensions. But as the bird gains strength, so does the beak gain size, and when it is adult the helmet and beak attain their full proportions. It is said that the age of the Hornbill may be known, by inspecting the beak, for that at every year a wrinkle is added to the number of furrows that are found on the bill.

The object of the huge helmet-like appendage is very obscure, but the probability is, that it may aid the bird in producing the loud roaring cry for which it is so celebrated. When at liberty in its native forests, the Hornbill is lively and active, leaping from bough to bough with great lightness, and appearing not to be in the least incommoded by its large beak. It ascends the tree by a succession of easy jumps, each of which bring it to a higher branch, and when it has attained the very summit of the tree, it stops and pours forth a succession of loud roaring sounds, which can be heard at a considerable distance.

COMMON TOUCAN.—*Rhamphastos Ariel.*

The very curious birds that go by the name of Toucans are not one whit less remarkable than the hornbills, their beak being often as extravagantly large, and their colours by far superior. They are inhabitants of America, the greater number of species being found in the tropical regions of that country.

Of these birds there are many species, of which no less than five were living in the Zoological Gardens in a single year. The voice of the Toucan is hoarse and rather disagreeable, and in many cases rather articulate

PARRAKEET COCKATOO.—*Nymphicus Novæ Hollandiæ.*

The general form of the Parrots is too well known to need description. All birds belonging to this large and splendid group can be recognised by the shape of their beaks, which are large, and have the upper mandible extensively curved and hanging far over the lower; in some species the upper mandible is of extraordinary length.

The Parrakeet Cockatoo is a native of Australia. It is mostly seen upon the ground, where it runs with great swiftness, and is very accomplished at winding its way among the grass stems, upon the seeds of which it subsists.

ROSE-HILL PARRAKEET.
Platycercus eximius.

The Rose-hill Parrakeet is found in New South Wales and Van Diemen's Land, and although very plentiful in places which it frequents, it is a very local bird, haunting one spot in hundreds, and then becoming invisible for a range of many miles. In the open country it lives in little companies like the preceding species, and is even more familiar, being exceedingly inquisitive, as is the nature of all the Parrot tribe. Plentiful as it is, there are few birds which are likely to suffer more from the gun, as its plumage is so magnificent and its form so elegant that it is in great request among the dealers, who are always sure of a sale when the beautiful skin is properly stuffed and put into a glass case.

The wings of the Rose-hill Parrakeet are not very powerful, and do not seem capable of enduring a journey of very great extent, for the bird always takes opportunities of settling as often as it can do so, and then after running along the ground for awhile, starts afresh. The flight is composed of a succession of undulations. The voice of this species is not so harsh as that of many Parrots, being a pleasing and not very loud whistle, which is often uttered. As the bird is a hardy one, and can bear confinement well, it is coming much into fashion as an inhabitant of the aviary, and will probably be brought over to England in great numbers.

The eggs of this bird are rather numerous, being from seven to ten as a general average, and they are laid in the hollow of some decaying gum-tree.

GROUND PARRAKEET.—*Pezophorus formósus.*

ALTHOUGH not endowed with the glowing hues of the preceding species, the GROUND PARRAKEET is a remarkably pretty and interesting bird. This species derives its name from its ground-loving habits. Mr. Gould says that it never perches on trees; but the author of "Bush Wanderings in Australia" remarks that he has seen it perching upon the tea-tree scrub. From its peculiarly pheasant-like shape and habits, it is sometimes called the pheasant by the colonists. It is a very common bird, and is found spread over many parts of Australia. Like that bird, it seldom takes to wing, but runs with great swiftness, winding its way rapidly among the rank grass and stems, and moving its limbs with such swiftness that they are almost as invisible as the spokes of a wheel in rapid motion.

When flushed, it only flies for a hundred yards or so, and then, if followed up, crouches closely to the ground, in hopes of being passed over. It makes its nest in some hollow tree.

BLUE-BANDED GRASS PARRAKEET.—*Euphémia Chrysóstoma.*

The Blue-banded Grass Parrakeet is also a native of Australia; and is not uncommon in the locality which it inhabits.

It is a summer visitor to Van Diemen's Land, where it remains from September to February or March. Thickly-wooded places are its only haunts, as it feeds almost wholly on seeds and grasses; and it is generally seen on the ground, unless it has been alarmed.

It congregates in flocks, and appears to have but little fear of danger, and but very odd notions of placing itself in safety; for, as soon as a flock is alarmed, all the birds flutter into the air, screaming feebly, and, after flying for a hundred yards or so, again alight. During the short time that they are on the wing, their flight is rapid, and very irregular, like that of the snipe.

The eggs of this bird are six or seven in number, and are mostly laid in the hole of a decaying gum-tree.

SCALY-BREASTED LORRIKEET.—*Trichoglossus chlorolepidótus.*

The Scaly-breasted Lorrikeet is a good example of a very large genus; and as the habits of all the species are very similar, more than a single example is not necessary. The name Trichoglossus signifies "hairy tongue," and is given to these birds in consequence of the structure of that member, which is furnished with bristly hairs, like the tongue of the honey-eaters, and is employed for the same purpose. This species may generally be found in those bush ranges which are interspersed with lofty gum-trees, from the blossoms of which it extracts the sweet juices on which it feeds. While employed in feeding, it clings so tightly to the blossoms, that if shot dead its feet will retain their hold. The amount of honey consumed by these birds is really surprising, a teaspoonful of honey having been taken from the crop of a single bird. Whenever the natives kill one of these birds, they always put its head in their mouths and suck the honey out of its crop. Young birds are always very well supplied with this sweet food, and are consequently in great favour with the native epicures.

When captured it is readily tamed, and is sufficiently hardy to live in a cage, provided that it be well supplied with sugar as well as seeds.

It assembles in large flocks of a thousand or more in number; and when one of the vast assemblies is seen perched on a tree, the effect is most magnificent.

This species will associate with others very harmoniously.

BLUE AND YELLOW MACAW.

Ara Ararauna.

THE MACAWS are mostly inhabitants of Southern America, in which country so many magnificent birds find their home.

They are all very splendid birds, and are all remarkable for their great size, their very long tails, and the splendid hues of their plumage. The beak is also very large and powerful, and, in some species, the ring round the eyes and part of the face is devoid of covering. Three species are well known in our menageries; but as their habits are all very similar, only one example has been figured. This is the great BLUE AND YELLOW MACAW, a bird which is mostly found in Demerara. It is a wood-loving bird, particularly haunting those places where the ground is wet and swampy, and where grows a certain palm, on the fruit of which it chiefly feeds.

The wings of this species are strong, and the long tail is so firmly set that considerable powers of flight are manifested. The Macaws often fly at a very high elevation, in large flocks, and are fond of executing sundry aërial evolutions before they alight. With one or two exceptions, they care little for the ground, and are generally seen on the summit of the highest trees.

Both parents assist in the duties of incubation.

GREY PARROT.—*Psittacus erythacus.*

The Grey Parrot has long been celebrated for its wonderful powers of imitation and its excellent memory.

It is a native of Western Africa, and is one of the commonest inhabitants of our aviaries, being brought over in great numbers by sailors, and always finding a ready sale as soon as the vessel arrives in port. Unfortunately the nautical vocabulary is none of the most refined, and the sailors have a malicious pleasure in teaching the birds to repeat some of the most startling of their phrases.

THE LOVE-BIRDS derive their name from the great fondness which they display for others of their own species, and the manner in which they always sit close to each other while perched, each trying to snuggle as closely as possible among the soft feathers of its neighbour.

They are all little birds, and among the smallest of these is the SWINDERN'S LOVE-BIRD, which measures barely six inches in length.

It is a rather scarce bird, but deserves notice on account of its very small dimensions, and its beautiful plumage. Like others of its kind, it is very fond of society, and unless furnished with a companion is very apt to droop, refuse nourishment, and die. Its habits in a wild state are not precisely known, as it is a bird of rare occurrence, and not easily to be watched.

The head of this species is light grass-green; round the back of the neck runs a black collar, and the chest, together with a band round the neck, just below the black collar, is yellow with a greenish cast. The general colour of the body is the same grass-green as that of the head, except the upper tail-coverts, which are deep rich azure. The short and rounded tail is beautifully and richly coloured, the two central feathers being green, and the others bright scarlet for the first half of their length, then banded with a warm bar of black, and the tips green. The bill is black, and of a stronger make than is usually the case with the Love-birds. The legs and feet are greyish black.

SWINDERN'S LOVE-BIRD.
Psittácula swinderniána.

GOLIATH ARATOO.—*Microglossum Aterrimum.*

The first of the Cockatoos which will be noticed in these pages is the Goliath Aratoo, a striking and very remarkable bird.

It is a native of New Guinea and the neighbouring islands, and is not a very common bird, although specimens may be found in several museums. The peculiar formation of the tongue and beak would lead the observer to suppose that its habits must be different from those of ordinary Cockatoos; but little or nothing is known of its mode of life in a wild state.

GREAT WHITE COCKATOO.—*Cacatúa Cristátus.*

Two species of Cockatoo are tolerably familiar in England, differing from each other in the colour of their crests.

The first of these is the GREAT WHITE COCKATOO, a remarkably handsome bird, especially when excited. In size it is rather a large bird, equalling a common fowl in dimensions, and assuming a much larger form when it ruffles up its feathers when under the influence of anger. Many of these birds are admirable talkers, and their voice is peculiarly full and loud.

SULPHUR-CRESTED COCKATOO.—*Cacatúa galerita*.

The species of Cockatoo which is most common in England is the SULPHUR-CRESTED COCKATOO, well depicted in the illustration. It may readily be distinguished from the preceding bird by the bright yellow colour of its crest and its more pointed form.

This bird is an inhabitant of different parts of Australia, and is especially common in Van Diemen's Land, where it may be found in flocks of a thousand in number.

LEADBEATER'S COCKATOO.—*Cacatúa Leadbeateri.*

The Leadbeater's Cockatoo is not so noisy as the common species, and may possibly prove a favourite inhabitant of our aviaries, its soft bluish-white plumage and splendid crest well meriting the attention of bird-fanciers. The crest is remarkable for its great development, and for the manner in which the bird can raise it like a fan over its head, or depress it upon the back of its neck at will. In either case it has a very fine effect, and especially so when it is elevated, and the bird excited with anger or pleasure.

PHILIP ISLAND PARROT.—*Nestor productus.*

A VERY singular form of Cockatoo is that which is known as the PHILIP ISLAND, or the LONG-BILLED PARROT.

This bird is only found in the little island from which it derives its name. It may probably become extinct at no distant period, as its singularly shaped beak renders it an object of attraction to those who get their living by supplying the dealers with skins and various objects of natural history; and its disposition is so gentle and docile that it readily accommodates itself to captivity.

OWL PARROT.—*Strigops habroptilus.*

The name given to the curious bird now before us is a very appropriate one as the creature seems to partake equally of the natures of the Owl and the Parrot.

Even in its habits it has much of the Owl nature, being as strictly nocturnal as any of those birds. During the daytime it conceals in holes. under the stumps of trees and similar localities, and seldom being seen except after sunset.

HAIRY-BREASTED BARBET.—*Laimodon Hirsútus.*

The Barbets form one of the groups into which the birds of the woodpecker tribe are divided.

The Hairy-Breasted Barbet is, perhaps, the most curious of all the Barbets, on account of the peculiarity from which it derives its name. The feathers of the breast are much stiffer than the others, and more sharply pointed; the shafts of the lower breast-feathers are devoid of web, and project to the distance of nearly an inch from the rest of the plumage, looking as if a number of long curved bristles had been inserted among the plumage.

All the Barbets possess strong and conical beaks, surrounded with bristles at the base, and their stiff tail-feathers enable them to support their bodies while they are perched upon the upright trunk of the tree on which they are seeking their insect food. They are all found in tropical climates, and the greater number, among which the present species may be included, are natives of Western Africa.

In their habits they are said to be rather slow and sluggish birds, not possessed of the fiery vivacity which distinguishes the true woodpeckers, and their food is not so wholly of an insect nature. The wings and tail are short, and all the species are of small dimensions.

The general colour of this bird is brown on the upper parts of the body, spotted with sulphur-yellow, a round mark of that tint being found on the end of each feather. The head, chin, and part of the throat are black, and there is one white stripe behind the eye, and another running from the angle of the mouth down the neck. The quill-feathers of the wings are deep brown, edged with sulphur-yellow.

GREAT SPOTTED WOODPECKER.

Picus major.

The GREAT SPOTTED WOODPECKER is a British species, and is also known by the name of Frenchpie and Woodpie.

It is found in many parts of England, and, like the other Woodpeckers, must be sought in the forests and woods rather than in orchards and gardens. Like other shy birds, however, it soon finds out where it may take up its abode unmolested, and will occasionally make its nest in some cultivated ground, where it has an instinctive assurance of safety, rather than entrust itself to the uncertain security of the forest.

In the woods frequented by these birds, which are often more plentiful than is generally known, the careful observer may watch their movements without difficulty, by taking a few preliminary precautions.

The rapid series of strokes on the bark, something like the sound of a watchman's rattle, will indicate the direction in which the bird is working; and when the intruding observer has drawn near the tree on which he suspects the Woodpecker to have settled, he should quietly sit or lie down, without moving. At first the bird will not be visible, for the Woodpeckers, like the squirrels, have a natural tact for keeping the tree-trunk or branch between themselves and the supposed enemy, and will not show themselves until they think that the danger has passed away. Presently the Woodpecker may be seen coming very cautiously round the tree, peering here and there, to assure itself that the coast is clear, and then, after a few preliminary taps, will set vigorously to work.

IVORY-BILLED WOODPECKER.—*Campéphilus principális.*

ALTHOUGH not the largest of the Woodpecker tribe, the IVORY-BILLED WOODPECKER, of North America, is perhaps the handsomest and most striking in appearance.

This splendid bird is armed with a tremendous beak, long, powerful, sharp, and white as ivory, which can be used equally as an instrument for obtaining its food, or as a weapon for repelling the attacks of its enemies, and, in the latter point of view, is a truly formidable arm.

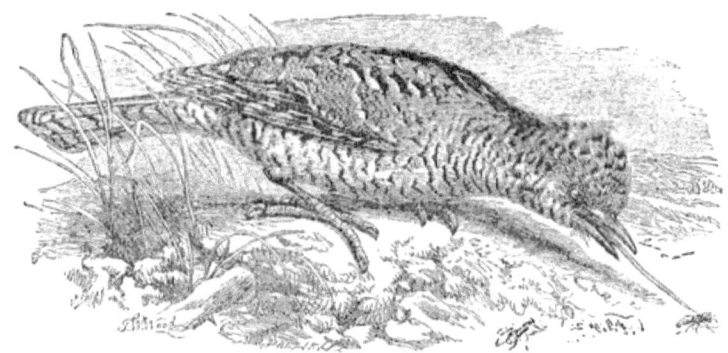

WRYNECK.—*Yunx touquilla*.

THE curious bird, known under the popular and appropriate name of the WRYNECK, is by some authors considered to be closely allied to the woodpeckers.

The Wryneck is a summer visitant to this country, appearing just before the cuckoo, and therefore known in some parts of England as the cuckoo's footman. There is a Welsh name for this bird, signifying "Cuckoo's knave," "Gwas-y-gôg," the pronunciation of which I must leave to Welsh throats.

The tongue of this bird is long and slender, and capable of being projected to the distance of an inch or so from the extremity of the beak, and its construction is almost exactly the same as that of the woodpecker. As might be supposed, it is employed for the same purpose, being used in capturing little insects, of which ants form its favourite diet. So fond, indeed, is the Wryneck of these insects, that in some parts of England it is popularly known by the name of Emmet-hunter. In pursuit of ants it trips nimbly about the trunks and branches of trees, picking them off neatly with its tongue as they run their untiring course. It also frequents ant-hills, especially when the insects are bringing out their pupæ to lie in the sun, and swallows ant and pupæ at a great pace. When, as in damp or cold weather, the ants remain within their fortress, the Wryneck pecks briskly at the hillock until it breaks its way through the fragile walls of the nest, and as the warlike insects come rushing out to attack the intruder of their home and to repair damages, make an excellent meal in spite of their anger and their stings.

When ants are scarce and scantily spread over the ground, the Wryneck runs after them in a very agile fashion; but when it comes upon a well stocked spot, it stands motionless, except the head, which is darted rapidly in every direction, the neck and part of the back twisting about like a snake.

GREAT HONEY GUIDE.—*Indicátor Major.*

The Honey Guides derive their name from the fact that they are extremely fond of wild bees and their honey, and by their eager cries attract keen-eared and sharp-eyed hunters to the spoil. It has been said that the birds intentionally ask the aid of mankind to dig out the nest where they commonly are placed in too secure a spot, and that they utter their peculiar cry of "cherr! cherr!" to call attention, and then precede their human assistants to the nest, fluttering their wings, and keeping a few yards in advance. That they do lead travellers to the bees' nest is true enough, but that they should seek out human beings, and intentionally bring them to the sweet stores seems doubtful, though it has been affirmed by many travellers.

One thing is certain, that the Honey Guide is by no means a safe conductor, as it sometimes leads its follower to the couching place of a lion, tiger, or the retreat of a poisonous snake. Gordon Cumming, as well as other travellers, testifies to this curious mode of conduct.

The feathers of the Honey Guide are thick, and the skin is tougher than is usually the case with birds, so that if the irritated bees should attack them, little harm is done, unless a sting should penetrate the eye or the bare skin around it.

Honey Guides are found in various parts of Africa, India, and Borneo, and in all cases their habits seem to be very similar.

PHEASANT CUCKOO.

Centropus Phasianus.

The Pheasant Cuckoo derives its popular and appropriate name from the great length of its tail, which gives to the bird an outline bearing some resemblance to that of the pheasant, a similitude which is further carried out by the bold markings of its plumage. This handsome bird is a native of New South Wales, where it is not uncommon, although rather a local bird, seldom wandering to any great distance from the spot which it loves.

It frequents low-lying and swampy lands, living almost entirely among the rank herbage of such localities, and keeping itself concealed among the brushes. When alarmed it flies to the nearest tree, alights on the lowest branches, rapidly makes its way through the boughs to the very summit, and then takes to wing.

The nest of this bird is placed on the ground, shaded by a convenient tuft of grass. It is a large and rather clumsily constructed edifice; having two apertures, through one of which the hen, while sitting, thrusts her head, and through the other she pokes her tail. The eggs are generally from three to five in number, and are more spherical than is generally the case among birds. Their colour is greyish-white, sometimes blotched with brown, and they are remarkable for the roughness of their shells.

SAVANNAH BLACKBIRD.—*Crotóphaga Ani.*

The Savannah Blackbird is rather a conspicuous bird, and is known by several other names, among which are Razor-billed Blackbird, and Great Blackbird. In some places it is called the Black Parrakeet, and in Mexico its native title is Cacalototl.

The food of the Savannah Blackbird is mostly of an animal nature, and consists chiefly of grasshoppers, locusts, and similar insects, although the bird is very fond of lizards and other small vertebrates, a prey which its peculiar beak is well calculated to secure. Seeds are also said to be eaten by this bird.

In some cases their insect-loving nature is directed in a manner very useful to cattle owners. In those regions, the cows are greatly troubled with ticks and other parasitic insects, which fasten upon their backs where the poor beasts cannot reach them. The Anis are fortunately very fond of these noxious insects, and perching upon the cow's back, soon rid them of their unpleasant companions. The cows are so well aware of the services rendered to them by these birds, that when they find themselves much annoyed by ticks, they lie down in order to permit the Anis to pursue their avocation without disturbance. Sometimes, according to Brown, in his "History of Jamaica," the Anis remind the cows of their reciprocal duties, and if the great quadruped forgets to lie down for their mutual benefit, they hop about just in front of its nose as it grazes, and give it no peace until it complies with their request.

CHANNEL BILL.—*Scythrops Novæ Hollandiæ.*

The very remarkable bird known by the name of Channel-Bill, inhabits part of Australia and some of the Eastern Islands. Its large and curiously-formed beak gives it so singular an aspect, that on a hasty glance it might almost be taken for a species of toucan or hornbill.

It is most common in New South Wales, and is migratory in its habits, arriving in October and departing in June. It is a gregarious bird, being seen in little flocks or companies varying in number from three to eight, and sometimes living in pairs. The voice of the Channel-Bill is by no means pleasing, and is exercised at the approach of rainy weather or the presence of a hawk. In either instance, the bird utters a series of vigorous yells, which are well understood by those who have studied its habits.

Its food consists of the seeds of the red gum and peppermint, and it also feeds upon beetles, phasmidæ, and other large insects of the land which it frequents.

CUCKOO.—*Cucúlus canórus.*

THE common CUCKOO is well known for its welcome chant, the sign that the colds of winter have passed away; and as an heartless mother, an abandoner of her offspring, and an occupier of other homes, it has been subjected to general reprobation. As is usual in such cases, both opinions are too sweeping; for the continual cry of "Cuck-oo! cuck-oo!" however agreeable it may be on the first hearing, soon becomes monotonous and fatiguing to the ear; and the mother Cuckoo is not so far lost to all feelings of maternity as to take no thought for her young, but ever remains near the place where it has deposited her egg, and seems to keep watch over the foster parents.

It is well known that the female Cuckoo does not make any nest, but places her egg in the nest of some small bird, and leaves it to the care of its unwitting foster-parents. Various birds are burdened with this charge, such as the hedge-warbler, the pied-wagtail, the meadow-pipit, the red-backed shrike, the blackbird, and various finches. Generally, however, the three first are those preferred.

Considering the size of the mother bird, the egg of the Cuckoo is remarkably small, being about the same size as that of the skylark, although the latter bird has barely one-fourth the dimensions of the former.

PASSENGER PIGEON.—*Ectopistes migratorius.*

AMONG the most extraordinary of birds, the PASSENGER PIGEON may take very high rank, not on account of its size or beauty, but on account of the extraordinary multitudes in which it sometimes migrates from one place to another. So vast are the flocks in which these birds assemble, that their numbers can barely be estimated by measurement. Wilson describes one flock of Passenger Pigeons to have been one mile in breadth, and two hundred and fifty miles long. He also calculates that this single flock would devour in one day seventeen million bushels of grain.

RING DOVE.—*Columba palumbus.*   STOCK DOVE.—*Columba œnas.*

The STOCK-DOVE derives its name from its habit of building its nest in the stocks or stumps of trees. It is one of our British Pigeons, and is tolerably common in many parts of England.

It is seldom found far northward, and even when it does visit such localities, it is only as a summer resident, making its nest in warmer districts. As has already been mentioned, the nest of this species is made in the stocks or stumps of trees, the birds finding out some convenient hollow, and placing their eggs within. Other localities are, however, selected for the purpose of incubation, among which a deserted rabbit-burrow is among the number.

The RING-DOVE is one of the commonest of our British birds, breeding in almost every little copse or tuft of trees, and inhabiting the forest grounds in great abundance. Towards, and during the breeding season, its soft complacent cooing—coo-goo-roo-o-o-o! coo-goo-roo-o-o-o—is heard in every direction, and with a very slight search its nest may be found.

GROUP.—DOMESTIC PIGEONS.—ROCK DOVE.—*Columbia Livia.*
BARBS.   CARRIERS.   POUTER.   NUNS.   TRUMPETERS.   BALD-HEAD.   TURBITS.
OWLS.   PANTAILS. JACOBINS.   TUMBLERS.

TOP KNOT PIGEON.—*Lopholäimus Antárcticus.*

The splendid Top-Knot Pigeon is one of the handsomest of the tribe, and in any collection of birds would be one of the most conspicuous species.

It is a native of southern and eastern Australia, and according to Mr. Gould, is most plentifully found in the bushes of the Illawarra and Hunter rivers. The powerful feet and general structure point it out as an arboreal bird, and it is so exclusively found in the trees that it will not even perch among the underwood, but must needs take its place on the branches of lofty trees.

TURTLE DOVE.—*Turtur Auritus.*

The world-famed Turtle-Dove, is, although a regular visitor of this country, better known by fame and tradition than by actual observation. The bird has, from classic time until the present day, been conventionally accepted as the type of matrimonial perfection, loving but its mate and caring for no other until death steps in to part the wedded couple.

Yet it is by no means the only instance of such conjugal affection among the feathered tribes, for there are hundreds of birds which can lay claim to the same excellent qualities, the fierce eagle and the ill-omened raven being among their number.

The nest of this bird is built lower than is generally the case with the Wood-Pigeon, and is usually placed on a forked branch of some convenient tree, about ten feet or so from the ground.

CROWNED PIGEON.—*Gaura Coronáta.*

The splendid Crowned Pigeon is indisputably the most conspicuous of all its tribe; its great size and splendid crest rendering it a most striking object, even at a considerable distance.

So large and so un-pigeon like is this bird, that few on first seeing it would be likely to determine its real relations to the rest of the feathered race, and would be more likely to class it among the poultry than the pigeons. It is a native of Java, New Guinea, and the Moluccas.

TOOTH-BILLED PIGEON.—*Didúnculus Strigirostris.*

In the Samoan islands of the Pacific is found a bird of extreme rarity and form, which is, as far as is known, unique among the feathered tribes that now inhabit the earth. I say, now inhabit, because in former days, when the Dodo was still in existence, that remarkable and ungainly bird presented a form and structure that were greatly similar to those of the Tooth-Billed Pigeon.

On account of its close relationship with the Dodo, it has received from some Zoologists, the generic name of Didunculus, or Little Dodo, while others have given it the title of Gnathodon, or Toothed-jaw, in allusion to the structure of its beak.

The food of this bird consists largely of the soft bulbous roots of several plants. The whole contour of the Tooth-bill is remarkable, and decidedly quaint; its rounded body seeming hardly in accordance with the large beak, which is nearly as long as the head, and is greatly arched on the upper mandible. The lower mandible is deeply cleft into three distinct teeth near its tip.

In colour it is rather a brilliant bird. The head, neck, breast, and abdomen are glossy greenish black, and upon the shoulders and the upper part of the back the feathers are velvety black, each having a crescent-shaped mark of shining green near its extremity

The total length of this bird is about fourteen inches.

DODO.—*Didus ineptus.*

The celebrated Dodo, once so common in the Mauritius, where it was discovered, is now considered to be wholly extinct, no living specimen having been known for very many years, and not even a stuffed skin being in existence. There are some relics of this bird, such as the head and a part of the jaw, and some similar specimens at the British Museum, but, excepting these, and one or two pictures, the Dodo has vanished from the visible world.

So plentiful were the Dodos at one time, and so easily were they killed, that the sailors were in the habit of slaying the birds merely for the sake of the stones in their stomachs, these being found very efficacious in sharpening their claspknives. The nest of the Dodo was a mere heap of fallen leaves gathered together on the ground, and the bird laid but one large egg. The weight of one full grown Dodo was said to be between forty and fifty pounds.

CRESTED CURASSOW.—*Crax Alector.*

THE CRESTED CURASSOW inhabits the thickly wooded districts of Guiana, Mexico, and Brazil, and is very plentifully found in those countries. It is really a handsome bird, nearly as large as the turkey, and more imposing in form and colour. It is gregarious in its habits, and assembles together in large troops, mostly perched on the branches of trees. It is susceptible of domestication, and, to all appearances, may be bred in this country, as well as the turkey or the pheasant.

In their native country the Curassows build among the trees, making a large and rather clumsy-looking nest of sticks, grass stems, leaves, and grass blades. There are generally six or seven eggs, not unlike those of the fowl, but larger and thicker shelled. The voice of the Crested Curassow is a short croak, but the various species differ slightly in this respect. The male Globose Curassow, for example, has a voice that sounds like a short hoarse cough, and every time that it utters the cry it jerks up its tail, and partially spreads the feathers.

BRUSH TURKEY.—*Tallegalla Lathami*.

The Brush Turkey is far from uncommon in many parts of New South Wales, and inhabits the densest bushes of that country. Like the Leipoa, when pursued it endeavours to effect its escape by running through the tangled brush, a feat which it can perform very adroitly; but it is not so silly as to allow itself to be taken by hand, as in the case of that bird. When very closely pursued, and unable to escape by speed, it jumps into the lowest branch of some tree, leaps from bough to bough, until it has reached the top, and either perches there or flies off to another part of the brush.

The nest of this bird is very remarkable, being composed of a huge mound of leaves, grasses, and such like materials, which are grasped in the large feet of the bird, and flung together in such quantities, that a single nest will sometimes contain several cartloads of material. The interior of this heap soon becomes hot, and the eggs are hatched by the warmth.

PEACOCK.—*Pavo cristátus.*

PEACOCKS.

The Peacock is an Asiatic bird, the ordinary species being found chiefly in India, and the Javanese Peacock in the country from which it derives its name. In some parts of India the Peacock is extremely common, flocking together in bands of thirty or forty in number, covering the trees with their splendid plumage, and filling the air with their horridly dissonant voices. Captain Williamson, in his "Oriental Field Sports," mentions that he has seen at least twelve or fifteen hundred peacocks within sight of the spot where he stood.

These birds are great objects of sport, and are mostly killed by the gun, though a good rider may sometimes run them down by fair chase. The Peacock takes some little preparation to get on the wing, and if hard pressed is not able to rise into the air. The horseman then strikes at the bird with his long lashed whip, so as to get the lash round its neck, and soon masters the beautiful quarry.

Peacock-shooting, although an exciting sport, is a dangerous one; the tiger feeling himself suited by the rhur and other vegetation in which the Peacock delights, so that an experienced sportsman may suddenly find himself face to face with a tiger, and run a strong chance of being himself the object of pursuit. Old hunters, however, who know the habits of the Peacock, find that bird extremely useful in denoting the presence of tigers. When the Peacock finds itself in close proximity to a tiger, or even a wild cat, it raises the sound of alarm, which is a loud hoarse cry, answered by those within hearing. The bird then utters a series of sharp, quick, grating notes, and gets higher into the trees, so as to be out of the reach of the tiger's claws.

In this country the Peacock is very common, and forms a magnificent addition to the lawn, the park, the garden, and the farmyard. The evident admiration and self-consciousness with which a Peacock regards himself are truly amusing, the bird always looking out for spectators before it spreads its train, and turning itself round and round, so as to display its beauties to the best advantage. At night it always roosts in some elevated spot, and invariably sits with its head facing the wind. Several Peacocks, whom I used to see daily, always roosted upon the thatch of a corn-rick, their long trains lying along the thatch so closely that towards dark they could hardly be seen. In character, the Peacock is as variable as other creatures, some individuals being mild and good-tempered, while others are morose and jealous to the extreme.

On the head of the Peacock is a tuft or aigrette of twenty-four upright feathers, blackish upon their almost naked shafts, and rich golden green shot with blue on their expanded tips. The top of the head, the throat and neck, are the most refulgent blue, changing, in different lights, to gold and green. On the back the feathers are golden green, edged with velvety black.

PHEASANT.—*Phasianus Colchicus.*

The Pheasant was originally brought into this country from Asia Minor, and by dint of careful preservation, has fairly settled itself in this country.

The food of this bird is extremely varied. When young it is generally fed on ants' eggs, maggots, grits, and similar food; but when it is fully grown, it is possessed of an accommodating appetite, and will eat many kinds of seeds, roots, and leaves. The tubers of the common buttercup form a considerable item in its diet, and the bird will also eat beans, peas, acorns, berries of various kinds, and has even been known to eat the ivy leaf as well as the berry.

The Pheasant is a ground-loving bird, running with great speed, and always preferring to trust to its legs rather than its wings.

The nest of this bird is merely a small heap of grass and leaves on the ground, on which are laid a large number of olive-brown eggs.

SILVER PHEASANT.—*Gallophásis Nycthémerus.*

GOLD PHEASANT.—*Thaumália picta.*

The Golden Pheasant is a native of China, where it is a great favourite not only for its splendid plumage and elegant form, but for the excellence of its flesh, which is said to surpass in delicacy even that of the common Pheasant.

For the purposes of the table, however, it is hardly likely to come into general use, as there are great difficulties in the way of breeding it in sufficient numbers.

It owes its name of Golden Pheasant to the rich golden ruff around its neck.

The Silver Pheasant is another inhabitant of China, and is found chiefly in the northern portions of that country.

It is one of the largest and most powerful of the tribe to which it belongs, and is said to be a match for a game-cock in fair combat. It is a hardy bird, and, like the Golden Pheasant, has been turned loose into British preserves, but with even less success.

BANKIVA FOWL.—*Gallus Bankiva.*—DOMESTIC FOWL.
COCHINS.   GAME.   BANTAMS.
SPANISH.   DORKINS.   POLISH.

DOMESTIC POULTRY.

We have here a group of the British Domestic Poultry, all of which are supposed to have descended from the Bankiva Jungle-fowl.

Towards the top, and on the left hand, may be seen some examples of the famous Cochin Fowl, whose enormous size and ungainly appearance took England so completely by storm some few years ago.

In the centre are a pair of the well-known game birds, formerly trained for fighting, but were kept on account of its good qualities as a domestic fowl. Even without training, it is very quarrelsome, and can attack and defend better than any other kind of fowl. So superior is it to the ordinary breeds in these respects, that I have seen a little old one-eyed Game-cock cut down, as if with a sword, a great swaggering barn-door cock that looked as if it could have killed its puny antagonist with a blow, and eaten him afterwards.

There seem to be no limits to the courage of the Game-cock, which will attack not only his own kind, but any other creature that may offend him.

Just below the game bird is seen an odd-looking fowl, with a head so covered with a monstrous plume of drooping feathers that its features are not more discernable than those of a skye-terrier under his thick hair. This wealth of plumage seems, however, to impoverish the brain, for the large-crested Polish fowls are generally stupid birds, and apt to meet with accidents which might easily be avoided.

On the opposite side of the plate is the Spanish fowl, a very fine variety, glossy black, with a very large comb, and notable for the white naked skin below the ear. It is a very large breed, coming next in size to the Cochin China, and very far surpasses that large but uncouth bird in the symmetry of its form. The flesh of this breed is excellent, and as the hens are regular layers, these birds are deservedly favourites among poultry owners.

On the foreground of the plate are some examples of those birds whose many excellencies have rendered a town famous. These are the Dorking Fowls, short-legged, round-bodied, plump-fleshed, and remarkable for having at least one, and sometimes two supplementary toes. These useful birds are mostly to be found in Surrey and Kent, the northern and marshy districts not suiting them. The Dorking Fowls are excellent for the table, their flesh being peculiarly plump and white, and the hens are remarkably prolific layers.

Lastly comes the odd, quaint, opiniated little Bantam, with its feathered legs, full breast, and bold fearless carriage. This minikin member of the poultry tribe is, despite his small dimensions, as bold as any of them, and if he thinks himself aggrieved will attack a great Cochin China or Spanish cock with spirited audacity.

TURKEY.—*Meleágris gallopavo.*

THE well-known TURKEY is properly a native of North America, where it is still very common in a wild state.

The female makes her nest in some secluded spot, and is very guarded in her approaches, seldom employing the same path twice in succession; and if discovered using various wiles by which to draw the intruder from the spot. As soon as the young are hatched she takes them under her charge, and the whole family go wandering about to great distances, at first returning to the nest for the night, but afterwards crouching in any suitable spot. Marshy places are avoided by the Turkey, as wet is fatal to the young birds until they have attained their second suit of clothes, and wear feathers instead of down. When they are about a fortnight old, they are able to get up into trees, and roost in the branches, safe from most of the numerous enemies which beset their path through life.

HONDURAS TURKEY.—*Meleágris Ocelláta.*

The splendid Honduras Turkey is even a more magnificent bird than the preceding species. It is found, as its name imports, in the wooded districts of Honduras and Yucatan.

Two specimens of this splendid bird, a male and female, were brought to the Zoological Gardens; and I am indebted to the kindness of Mr. T. W. Wood, the artist of the accompanying illustration, for the following short account of its habits in a state of captivity, I being at the time unable through ill health to visit the gardens. "In the spring, the male became highly excited, and stalked about with his tail spread, wings drooping, and all his feathers puffed up, looking as if he would burst with pride. At such a time his head was thrown back so far and his breast-feathers projecting so far that he could not observe the ground beneath him, and consequently he often stepped into the water, much to his annoyance and the visitor's amusement."

GUINEA FOWL.—*Númida Meleagris.*

THE GUINEA FOWL or PINTADO is well known in our farmyards.

Both in the wild and the captive state the Guinea Fowl is wary and suspicious, and particularly careful not to betray the position of its nest, thus often giving great trouble to the farmer. Sometimes when the breeding season approaches, the female Pintado will hide herself and nest so effectually that the only indication of her proceedings is her subsequent appearance with a brood of young round her. The number of eggs is rather large, being seldom below ten and often double that number. Their colour is yellowish-red, covered with very little dark spots, and their size is less than that of the common fowl. Their shells are extremely hard and thick, and when boiled for the table require some little exertion to open properly.

This bird has been imported into America and several of the West Indian islands, where it has entirely acclimatised itself.

PARTRIDGE.—*Perdrix Cinereus*.

The Common Partridge is found spread over the greater part of Europe, always being found most plentifully near cultivated ground. In all probability this bird, although it may do some damage to the corn-fields, may still be very useful to the farmer by its unceasing war upon the smaller "vermin" that devastate the fields and injure the crops. Small slugs are a favourite diet with the Partridge, which has a special faculty for discovering them in the recesses where they hide themselves during the day, and can even hunt successfully after the eggs of these destructive creatures. Caterpillars are also eaten by this bird, and the terrible black grub of the turnip is consumed in great numbers by the Partridges. Even the white cabbage butterfly, whose numerous offspring are so hurtful to the kitchen garden, falls a victim to the quick-eyed Partridge, which leaps into the air and seizes it in its beak as the white-winged pest comes fluttering unsuspectingly over the bird's head.

The Partridge begins to lay about the end of April, gathering together a bundle of dried grasses, into some shallow depression in the ground, and depositing therein a clutch of eggs, generally from twelve to twenty in number. Sometimes a still greater number have been found, but, in these cases, it is tolerably evident, from many observations, that several birds have laid in the same nest.

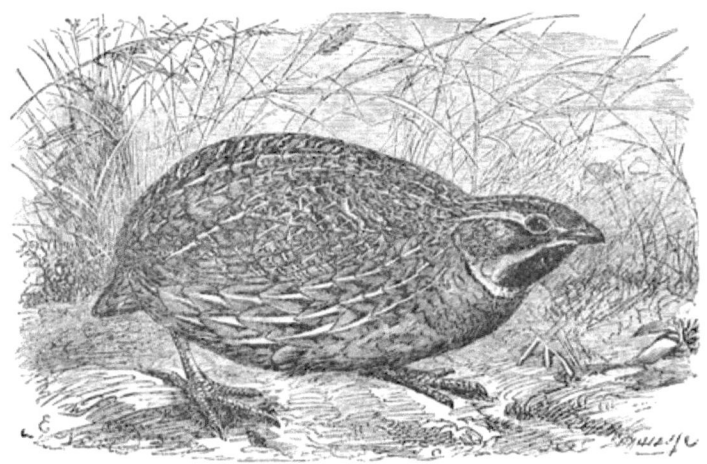

QUAIL.—*Coturnix Communis.*

The odd, short-legged, round-bodied, quick-footed Quail is closely allied to the partridge in form and many of its habits. Of these birds there are many species; but as all are much alike, there is no need of many examples.

The common Quail is found spread over the greater part of Europe, and portions of Asia and Africa, coming to our island in the summer, though not in very great numbers. In England the bird is not sufficiently plentiful to be of any commercial value, but in Italy, and some of the warmer lands which the Quails traverse during their periodical migrations, the inhabitants look forward to the arrival of the Quail with the greatest anxiety. In those countries they are shot, snared, and netted by thousands; and it is chiefly from the foreign markets that our game shops are supplied with these birds. When fat the flesh of the Quail is very delicious; and the most approved way of cooking the bird is to envelop it in a very thin slice of bacon, tie it up in a large vine-leaf, and then roast it.

In their migrations the Quails fly by night, a peculiarity which has been noted in the Scriptural record of the Exodus, where it is mentioned that "at even the Quails came up and covered the camp."

The nest of the Quail is of no better construction than that of the partridge. The number of eggs is generally about fourteen or fifteen.

CAPERCAILLIE.—*Tetrao Urogallus*

ALTHOUGH once a common inhabitant of the highland districts of Great Britain, the CAPERCAILLIE has now been almost wholly extinct for some years, a straggling specimen being occasionally seen in Scotland, and shot for the benefit of science.

This bird is also known by the following names: Cock of the woods, Mountain Cock, Auerhahn, and Capercailzie.

It is now most frequently found in the northern parts of Europe, Norway and Sweden being very favourite homes.

The Capercaillie is celebrated, not only for its great size and the excellence of its flesh, but for its singular habits just previous to and during the breeding season.

RUFFED GROUSE.—*Tetrao umbellus.*

The Ruffed Grouse is an American bird, and has some of the habits of the preceding species. Wilson writes as follows of it:—

"In walking through the solitary woods frequented by these birds, a stranger is surprised by suddenly hearing a kind of thumping very similar to that produced by striking two full-blown bladders together, but much louder. The strokes at first are slow and distinct, but gradually increase in rapidity, till they run into each other, resembling the rumbling sound of very distant thunder, dying away gradually on the ear. It is produced in the following manner:—

"The bird, standing on an old prostrate log, generally in a retired and sheltered situation, lowers his wings, erects his expanded tail, contracts his throat, elevates the tufts of feathers on the neck, and inflates his whole body, something in the manner of the turkey-cock, strutting and wheeling about with great stateliness."

WHITE SHEATH-BILL.—*Chionis alba.*

ANOTHER curious group of birds is known by the title of Sheath-bills, on account of the remarkable sheath of horny substance, which is situated on the base of the bill, and under which lie the nostrils.

One of the commonest species of this group is the WHITE SHEATH-BILL, a native of Australia, New Zealand, and neighbouring islands.

This bird is seen upon the coasts, finding its food among the molluscs, small crustaceæ, fish, and other similar substances. Perhaps, under some circumstances, it may subsist on carrion, and thereby give an evil flavour to its flesh, as there are very contradictory reports as to its value for the table, some specimens having been of so vile an odour that even the sailors could not touch the ill-savoured flesh, while, in other cases, the bird is reported to be of excellent quality, and equal to duck in tenderness and flavour.

OSTRICH.—*Strúthio Camélus.*

The Ostrich, which is placed at the head of the Running Birds, is a native of Southern Africa.

EMEU.—*Dromaius Novæ Hollándiæ.*

The Emeu is a native of Australia. It much resembles the ostrich, and has many of its habits. Its flesh is thought to be very good, and by the natives is only permitted to the men, the women and children not being allowed to eat it.

CASSOWARY.—*Casuárius Emu.*

The Cassowary inhabits the Malaccas. This fine bird is remarkable for the helmet-like projection on the head, and the character of the feathers.

The plumage of the body is very hair-like, being composed of long and almost naked shafts, two springing from the same tube, and one always being longer than the other. At the roots of the shafts there is a small tuft of delicate down, sufficiently thick to supply a warm and soft inner garment, but yet so small as to be hidden by the long hair-like plumage. Even the tail is furnished with the same curious covering, and the wings are clothed after a similar manner, with the exception of five black, stiff, strong, pointed quills, very like the large quills of the porcupine, and being of different lengths, the largest not exceeding one foot, and generally being much battered about the point. When stripped of its feathers, the whole limb only extends some three inches in length. An adult male is about three feet in height.

APTERYX.—*Apteryx austrális.*

The Kiwi-kiwi, or Apteryx, is a native of New Zealand, where it was once very common, but is now become scarce.

In this bird there is scarcely the slightest trace of wings, a peculiarity which has gained for it the title of Apteryx, or wingless. The plumage is composed of rather curiously-shaped flat feathers, each being wide and furnished with a soft, shining, silken down for the basal third of its length, and then narrowing rapidly towards the extremity, which is a single shaft, with hair-like webs at each side. The quill portion of the feathers is remarkably small and short, being even overlapped by the down when the feather is removed from the bird.

The skin is very tough and yet flexible, and the chiefs set great value upon it for the manufacture of their state mantles, permitting no inferior person to wear them, and being extremely unwilling to part with them even for a valuable consideration.

GREAT BUSTARD.—*Otis tarda.*

The Great Bustard was once quite common in this country, but is now very seldom seen.

This splendid bird, although in former days quite an usual tenant of plains and commons, and having been an ordinary object of chase on Newmarket Heath, is now so very rare, that an occasional specimen only makes its appearance at very rare intervals, and is then generally found—and shot—on Salisbury Plain. Its general colour is ches'nut, barred with black, the head and neck are grey, and the under surface white.

GOLDEN PLOVER.—*Charádrius Pluviális.*
DOTTEREL.—*Charádrius morinellus.*
KENTISH PLOVER.—*Charádrius Cantiánus.*

THREE English PLOVERS are seen in this illustration.

The GOLDEN PLOVER, sometimes called the YELLOW PLOVER from its prettily coloured plumage, is common in many parts of England, being found mostly in the more northern districts of Great Britain. Its colour is greyish-black above, mottled with golden-yellow, and the face, chin, and under parts, are black.

The DOTTEREL has long been held as the type of stupidity, and to call a man a Dotterel is considered as great an insult as to term him a goose or a donkey. Its colour is brown of various shades, mottled with white.

The pretty little KENTISH PLOVER may be seen on some of our shores, running along the edge of the waves with surprising celerity.

TURNSTONE.—*Cinclus intérpres.*

The handsomely plumed Turnstone is, though a little bird, so boldly decorated with black, white, and ruddy orange, that it is more conspicuous upon the coast than birds of double its size.

The name is derived from its movements when feeding, at which times it runs along the beech, picking up sandhoppers, marine worms, and other creatures, and turning over the stones in its course for the purpose of getting at the small crustaceæ that are generally found in such situations. This bird is spread over a considerable portion of the world, and is found even in Northern America, where it retains the same habits which distinguish it in Europe.

According to Wilson, it feeds almost wholly, during May and June, on the spawn of the king-crab, and is known by the name of the Horse-foot Snipe, the king-crab being popularly called the horse-foot crab. It runs with some speed, but not the rapidity that characterizes many shore-loving birds, and spends some time in examining any spot of ground to which it has taken a fancy, tossing the pebbles from side to side, and picking up the unfortunate being that may have lain under their shelter. The nest of this bird is situated upon the coast, and the bird is very valiant in its attacks upon the gulls which approach too near its home. A nest found by Mr. Hewitson " was placed against a ledge of rock, and consisted of nothing more than the drooping leaves of the juniper-bush, under a creeping branch, by which the eggs, four in number, were snugly concealed, and admirably sheltered from the many storms by which these bleak and exposed rocks are visited, allowing just sufficient room for the bird to cover them."

It is a beautiful bird, boldly marked with black and white.

CARIAMA. GOLDEN-BREASTED TRUMPETER.
Cariáma cristáta. *Psophia crépitans.*

BOTH these birds are natives of tropical America.

The GOLDEN-BREASTED TRUMPETER is a handsome bird, remarkable for the short velvety feathers of the head and neck, and their beautiful golden green lustre on the breast.

The name of Trumpeter is derived from the strange hollow cry which it utters without seeming to open the beak.

The CARIAMA is rather larger than the trumpeter, and has many of the same habits. It is chiefly remarkable for the feathery crest on the crown and forehead.

It is easily tamed, and soon becomes so attached to its new home that it is accustomed to roam about at will, and to return to its owner like the common fowl.

CRANE.—*Grus cinérea*.

ALTHOUGH in former days tolerably common in England, the CRANE has now, with the bustard, almost disappeared from this land, a single specimen being seen at very long and increasing intervals. In some parts of England and Ireland the popular name of the heron is the Crane, so that the occasional reports which sometimes find admission into local newspapers respecting the Crane have often reference, not to that bird, but to the heron.

The Crane is found in various parts of the continent of Europe, migrating from place to place, and flying in large flocks at a great elevation in the air. They continue their aerial journeys for great distances, and seldom descend but for the purpose of feeding.

The Crane makes its nest mostly on marshy ground, placing it among osiers, reeds, or the heavy vegetation which generally flourishes in such localities. The eggs are two in number, and their colour is light olive, covered with dashes of a deeper hue and brown.

DEMOISELLE CRANE.—*Scops Virgo.*
CROWNED CRANE.—*Balearica pavonina.*

These two birds are remarkable, not only for their beauty of form and plumage, but for the extraordinary antics in which they occasionally indulge.

The Demoiselle, or Numidian Crane, is common in many parts of Africa, and has been seen in some portions of Asia, and occasionally in Eastern Europe. The movements of this beautiful bird are generally slow and graceful, with a certain air of delicate daintiness about them which have earned for it the title of Demoiselle. But on occasions it is seized with a fit of eccentricity, and puts itself through a series of absurd gambols, dancing about on the tip of its toes, flapping its wings, and bowing its head in the most grotesque fashion.

The Crowned Crane is even more striking than the Demoiselle, its coronet of golden plumes, and the scarlet cheeks making it a very conspicuous bird.

BITTERN.—*Botaurus stellaris.*　　HERON.—*Ardea cinerea.*　　EGRETT.—*Ardea egretta.*

THREE examples of the HERONS we give in this illustration.

The EGRET is a native of several parts of America, having its principal residence in the southern portions of that continent, and visiting the more northern districts during several months of the year, arriving generally about February or March. As it finds its food among inundated and swampy grounds, it is generally seen haunting the rice-fields, the marshy river-shores, and similar localities, and seldom, if ever, visits the high inclosed regions. The food of the Egret consists of the smaller mammalia, little fish, frogs, lizards, snakes, and insects. It is a handsome and elegant bird, and is conspicuous among the low marshy grounds which it frequents, on account of its large size and snowy plumage.

The HERON still holds its place among the familiar British birds, being found on the banks of almost every river and lake. It feeds mostly upon fish, frogs, and similar creatures.

While engaged in its search for food, the Heron stands on the water's edge, mostly with its feet or foot immersed, and there remains still as if carved out of wood, with its neck retracted, and its head resting between the shoulders. In this attitude its sober plumage and total stillness render it very inconspicuous, and as it mostly prefers to stand under the shadow of a tree, bush, or bank, it cannot be seen except by a practised eye, in spite of its large size. The back view of the bird while thus standing partakes largely of the ludicrous, and reminds the observer of a large jargonelle pear with a long stalk stuck in the ground. Sometimes it likes to squat on its bent legs, the feet being pushed out in front, and the knees, or rather ankles bent under its body. It generally suns itself in this position, partially spreading the wings and slightly shaking them. Usually it sits with the head resting on the shoulders; but if alarmed at any unexpected sound, it shuts its wings, stretches its neck to the utmost extent, and then presents a most singular aspect.

The flight of the Heron is grand and stately, for the wings are long and wide, and, in spite of the outstretched neck and the counterbalancing legs, the bird moves through the air with a noble and rapid flight. It is curious to see a Heron pass directly overhead. The long neck, body, and legs, are stretched in a line, stiff and immovable, and the gently waving wings carry the bird through the air with a rapidity that seems the effect of magic.

The long beak of the Heron is very sharp and dagger-like, and can be used with terrible force as an offensive weapon. The bird instinctively aims its blow at the eye of its adversary, and, if incautiously handled, is sure to deliver a stroke quick as lightning at the captor's eye.

The BITTERN is now seldom seen in this country, partly because it is a rare bird and becoming scarcer almost yearly, and partly because its habits are nocturnal. In habits and food the Bittern resembles the heron, except that it feeds by night instead of by day.

SPOONBILL.—*Platalea leucoródia.*

The curious Spoonbill has a very wide range of country, being spread over the greater part of Europe and Asia, and inhabiting a portion of Africa. Like the birds to which it is closely allied, this species is one of the waders, frequenting the waters, and obtaining a subsistence from the fish, reptiles, and smaller aquatic inhabitants, which it captures in the broad spoon-like extremity of its beak. It is also fond of frequenting the sea-shore, where it finds a bountiful supply of food along the edges of the waves and in the little pools that are left by the retiring waters, where shrimps, crabs, sand-hoppers, and similar animals, are crowded closely together as the water sinks through the sand. The bird also eats some vegetable substances, such as the roots of aquatic herbage, and when in confinement will feed upon almost any kind of animal or vegetable matter, providing it be soft and moist.

STORK.—*Cicónia Alba.*

The Stork is another of the birds which, in olden days, were tolerably frequent visitors to the British Islands, but which now seldom make their appearance in such inhospitable regions, where food is scarce and guns are many.

It is sufficiently common in many parts of Europe, where it migrates yearly from its winter quarters in Africa, makes its nest and rears its young. In some countries it is rigidly protected by common consent, on account of the service which it renders in the destruction of noisome reptiles and unpleasant offal.

ADJUTANT.—*Leptoptilus Argála.*

THE well-known ADJUTANT or ARJALA is a native of India.

This fine bird is notable for the enormous size of the beak, which is capable of seizing and swallowing objects of considerable size, a full-grown cat, a fowl, or a leg of mutton being engulfed without any apparent difficulty.

WHALE-HEADED STORK.—*Balæniceps Rex.*

THE singular WHALE-HEADED STORK is the most striking of its tribe.

This bird lives in Northern Africa, near the Nile, but is seldom seen on the banks of that river, preferring the swampy districts to the running water. Mr. Petherick, who first brought this bird to England, found it in the Rhol district, in a large tract of country about a hundred and fifty miles in extent, where the ground is continually swelled by rains, and has by degrees modified into a huge morass, some parts flooded with water, others blooming with vegetation, and the whole surrounded by thick bush.

It feeds upon fish and water snakes, and will also tear open the carcases of dead animals with its strong hooked bill.

The chief point in this fine bird is the huge bill, which, from its resemblance in size and shape to a shoe, has gained for its owner the title of Shoe-bird. It is enormously expanded at each side of the beak, the edges of the upper mandible overhang those of the lower, and its tip is furnished with a large hook, curved and sharp as that of an eagle.

SACRED IBIS.—*Ibis religiósa.*   GLOSSY IBIS.—*Ibis falcinellus.*

The Sacred Ibis is so called because it figures largely in an evidently sacred character on the heiroglyphics of ancient Egypt. It is a migratory bird, arriving in Egypt as soon as the waters of the Nile begin to rise, and remaining in that land until the waters have subsided, and therefore deprived it of its daily supplies of food. The bird probably owes its sacred character to the fact that its appearance denotes the rising of the nile, an annual phenomenon on which depends the prosperity of the whole country.

Another species, the Glossy Ibis, is also an inhabitant of Northern Africa, but is sometimes found in this country, where the fishermen know it by the name of Black Curlew. It is probably the Black Ibis mentioned by Herodotus.

The Glossy Ibis is sometimes found in different parts of America, rarely in the northern States, but of more frequent occurence in the centre or south.

Its food consists mostly of molluscs, both terrestrial and aquatic, but it will eat worms, insects, and probably the smaller reptiles.

CURLEW.—*Numénius arquáta.*   WHIMBREL.—*Numénius phœpus.*

The Curlew, or Whaup, is mostly found upon the sea-shore and upon moorlands, and partly on account of its wild shy habits, and partly because its flesh is very delicate and well flavoured, is greatly pursued by the sportsmen. These birds are most annoying to a gunner who does not understand their ways, having a fashion of keeping just out of gun range, rising from the ground with a wild mournful cry which has the effect of alarming every other bird within hearing, and flying off to a distance, where they alight only to play the same trick again.

At first sight the Whimbrel looks something like a diminutive curlew, save that the bill is not so long, so thick, nor so sharply curved as in the preceding species. On account of this resemblance it is in some places known by the name of Half-Curlew and in others it is called the Jack Curlew. In the Shetland Isles it is known by the popular name of Tang-Whaap.

The habits of the Whimbrel much resemble those of the curlew.

KNOT.—*Tringa canutus.*   TEMMINCK'S STINT.—*Tringa Temminckii.*
PIGMY CURLEW.—*Tringa subarquata.*   DUNLIN.—*Tringa cinclus.*

The Knot is found upon our coast in varying numbers, at one season flying and settling on the shore in flocks of a thousand or more in number, and at another being so scarce that hardly one bird can be seen where a hundred had formerly made their appearance.

The Pigmy Curlew, or Curlew Sandpiper, is so called on account of the form of its beak, which bears some resemblance to that of the Curlew, although it is much smaller and not so sharply curved.

Temminck's Stint is remarkable for being the smallest of the British Sandpipers, the average length being about five inches and a half.

The Dunlin is the commonest of the sea-loving Sandpipers, and comes to our shores in large flocks, keeping close to the edge of the waves, running along the sands and pecking eagerly at the molluscs, worms, and smaller crustacea, which are so plentiful on the margin of the retiring waves.

JACK SNIPE.—*Gallinágo gallinula.*   COMMON SNIPE.—*Galliná média.*

The little Jack Snipe is seldom seen in this country, except in the winter, and is remarkable for its tenacity in clinging to the ground even on the near approach of an enemy. Terror seems to have some part in the propensity, for Mr. Yarrell remarks that a Jack Snipe has allowed itself to be picked up by hand before the nose of a pointer.

The plumage of the Jack Snipe is very like that of the common species, but may be at once distinguished by the absence of the pale brown streak over the top of the head.

The Common Snipe is too well known to need much description. Its habits, however, are interesting, and deserve some notice.

The male bird has a curious habit of rising to a great height in the air, circling repeatedly over the same ground, and uttering continually a peculiar cry, like the words "chic! chic! chic-a, chic-a, chic-a," constantly repeated.

JACANA.—*Parra Jacana.*

The Jacanas are remarkable for the extraordinary development of their toes, which are so long and so slender that they seem to have been drawn out like wire, and to impede the progress of their owner. These elongated toes are, however, of the greatest use, as they enable the bird to walk upon the floating leaves which overspread the surface of many rivers, and to pick its food from and between the leaves on which it walks. As the bird marches upon the leaves, the long toes dividing the pressure upon several leaves at each step, they are slightly sunk below the surface by the weight, so that the bird appears to be really walking upon water.

The Common Jacana is a native of Southern America, and there are other species scattered over Africa, Asia, and Australia.

Mr. Gould tells us that the Australian species is a good diver, but a bad flier. "Their powers of diving and of remaining under water are equal to those of any bird I have ever met with; on the other hand, the powers of flight are very weak. They will, however, mount up fifteen or twenty yards and fly from one end of the lake to the other, a distance of half or three-quarters of a mile; but generally they merely rise above the surface of the water, and fly off for about a hundred yards. During flight their long legs are thrown out horizontally to their full length. While feeding, they utter a slowly-repeated 'cluck, cluck.' The stomach is extremely muscular, and the food consists of aquatic insects and some kind of vegetable matter."

HORNED SCREAMER.
Palamedéa cornuta.

CRESTED SCREAMER.
Chauná chaváría.

The Horned Screamer, or Kamichi, is a native of Central America, and is found in the vast swamps and morasses of that hot and moist country, where the vegetation springs up in gigantic luxuriance and the miasmatic morasses give birth to reptiles and creeping things innumerable. The large spurs on the wings are valuable to the bird in repelling the attacks of the numerous snakes, and guarding itself and young from their rapacity.

Another well-known example, the Crested Screamer, or Chaja, is a finer-looking bird than the preceding species, though its head is without the singular appendage that gives the Horned Screamer so singular an aspect. The name of Chaja is given to this bird on account of its cry, that of the male bird being "chaja" and of the female "chajali." It is a native of Brazil and Paraguay, and is generally found near the banks of rivers.

WATER RAIL.—*Rallus aquaticus.*

The Water Rail is but seldom seen, partly because it really is not very plentiful, and partly on account of its shy and retiring habits, and its powers of concealment. It frequents ponds, lakes, and similar localities, haunting those places where luxuriant reed-beds afford it shelter and covert. On the least alarm it sets off for the place of refuge, diving to a considerable distance and always pressing towards the reeds, through which it glides with wonderful address, and is immediately out of danger. Even a trained dog can hardly flush a Water Rail when once it has reached its reedy refuge. The food of the Water Rail consists of insects, worms, leeches, molluscs, and similar creatures.

CORNCRAKE, OR LANDRAIL.—*Ortygometra crex.*

The well-known Corncrake, or Landrail, is common in almost every part of the British Islands, its rough grating call being heard wherever the hay-grass is long enough to hide the utterer.

FLAMINGO.—*Phœnicópterus ruber.*

The common Flamingo is plentiful in many parts of the Old World, and may be seen in great numbers on the sea-shore, or the banks of large and pestilential marshes, the evil atmosphere of which has no effect upon this bird, though to many animals it is most injurious, and to man a certain death. When feeding the Flamingo bends its neck, and placing the upper mandible of the curiously bent beak on the ground or under the water, separates the nutritive portions with a kind of spattering sound, like that of a duck when feeding. The tongue of the Flamingo is very thick, and of a soft oily consistence, covered with curved spines pointing backwards, and not muscular.

A flock of these birds feeding along the sea-shore have a curious appearance, bending their long necks in regular succession as the waves dash upon the shore, and raising them as the ripple passes away along the strand.

The colour of the Flamingo is scarlet, with black wings.

GREY-LAG GOOSE.—*Anser ferus.*   BEAN GOOSE.—*Anser segetum.*

The Grey-lag Goose is the stock from which our domestic geese has been derived.

In a state of domestication the Goose lives to a great age, and when treated kindly becomes strongly attached to its friends, and assumes quite an eccentric character. Of the breeding and management of the Goose nothing can be said in these pages, the reader being referred to the numerous works on domestic poultry.

The Grey-Lag Goose may be known by the pinky bill, with its white horny nail at the tip of the mandible. The head, nape, and upper part of the back are ashen brown, and the lower part of the back bluish grey.

The Bean Goose is another of our English examples of this genus, but it is only a visitant of our shores, having its chief residence in the Arctic circle and high northern latitudes, and coming southward about October.

BLACK SWAN.—*Cynus atrátus.*

The Black Swan is now quite common in England, though in former times it was thought to be an impossible bird.

This fine bird comes from Australia, where it was first discovered in 1698. It is a striking and handsome bird, the blood-red bill and the white primaries contrasting beautifully with the deep black of the plumage. It is not so elegant in its movements as the white Swan, and holds its neck stiffly, without the easy serpentine grace to which we are so well accustomed in our British Swans. The young are not unlike those of the white Swan, and are covered with a blackish grey down.

It is a very prolific bird, producing two and sometimes three broods in a season, commencing to breed about October, and ceasing at the middle of January. The nest is like that of the Swan's, and the eggs are from five to eight in number, of a pale green, washed with brown.

MANDARIN DUCK—*Aïx galericuláta.*

The beautiful Mandarin Duck is worthy of heading the true Ducks, for a more magnificently clothed bird can hardly be found when the male is in health and in his full nuptial plumage.

These birds are natives of China, and are held in such esteem that they can hardly be obtained at any price, the natives having a singular dislike to seeing their birds pass into the possession of Europeans. "A gentleman," writes Dr. Bennett, "very recently wrote from Sydney to China, requesting some of these birds to be sent to him. The reply was, that from the present disturbed state of China, it would be easier to send him a pair of mandarins than a pair of Mandarin Ducks." This bird has the power of perching, and it is a curious sight to watch them perched on the branches of trees overhanging the water.

The crest of this beautiful Duck is varied green and purple upon the top of the head, the long crest-like feathers being chestnut and green. From the eye to the beak the colour is warm fawn, and a stripe from the eye to the back of the neck is soft cream.

MALLARD.—*Anas boschas.*

The common Mallard, or Wild Duck, is a truly handsome bird.

It is the stock from which is descended our well-known domestic Duck, to which we are so much indebted for its flesh and its eggs.

In its wild state the Mallard arrives in this country about October, assembling in large flocks, and is immediately persecuted in every way that the ingenuity of man can devise. Sportsmen go out to shoot it, armed with huge guns that no man can hold to his shoulder, and have to be mounted on gimbals in a boat, thus bringing down whole clouds of birds at a discharge.

The nest of the Mallard is made of grass, lined and mixed with down, and is almost always placed on the ground near water, and sheltered by reeds, osiers, or other aquatic plants. Sometimes, however, the nest is placed in a more inland spot, and it now and then happens that a duck of more than usual eccentricity builds her nest in a tree at some elevation from the ground, so that when her young are hatched, she is driven to exert all her ingenuity in conveying them safely from their lofty cradle to the ground or the water. Such a nest has been observed in an oak-tree twenty-five feet from the ground, and at Heath-wood, near Chesterford, one of these birds usurped possession of a deserted crow's nest in an oak-tree. Many similar instances are on record.

The eggs are rather large and of a greenish white colour.

EIDER DUCK.—*Somatéria mollissima.*

In the southern parts of England the Eider Duck is only a winter visitant, but remains throughout the year in the more northern portions of our island, and in the north of Scotland.

This bird is widely celebrated on account of the exquisitely soft and bright down which the parent plucks from its breast and lays over the eggs during the process of incubation. Taking these nests is with some a regular business, not devoid of risk, on account of the precipitous localities in which the Eider Duck often breeds. The nest is made of fine seaweeds, and after the mother-bird has laid her complement of eggs she covers them with the soft down, adding to the heap daily until she completely hides them from view.

The plan usually adopted is to remove both eggs and down, when the female lays another set of eggs and covers them with fresh down. These are again taken, and then the male is obliged to give his help by taking down from his own breast, and supplying the place of that which was stolen. The down of the male bird is pale coloured, and as soon as it is seen in the nest, the eggs and down are left untouched in order to keep up the breed.

The Eider is a shy retiring bird, placing its nest on islands and rocks projecting well into the sea. It is an admirable diver, its legs being set very far back, and obtains much of its food by gathering it under water.

GREAT NORTHERN DIVER.—*Colymbus glaciális.*

The Great Northern Diver is found on the northern British coasts, and may be seen disporting itself in the water with astonishing activity.

Perhaps there is no bird which excels the Northern Diver in its powers of swimming, although the penguins and cormorants are equally notable in that respect. Its broad webbed feet are set so very far back that the bird cannot walk properly, but tumbles and scrambles along much after the fashion of a seal, pushing itself with its feet, and scraping its breast on the ground. In the water, however, it is quite at its ease, and, like the seal, no sooner reaches the familiar element, than it dives away at full speed, twisting and turning under the surface as if in the exuberance of happy spirits. So swiftly can it glide through the water, that it can chase and capture the agile fish in their own element.

The eggs of the Northern Diver are generally two in number, and of a dark olive-brown, spotted sparingly with brown of another tone.

EARED GREBE. GREAT CRESTED GREBE.
Podiceps aurítus. *Podiceps cristátus.*

The Great Crested Grebe is found throughout the year in several parts of England, preferring the lakes and the fenny districts. Like the divers, the Grebes are very bad walkers, but wonderfully active in the water, and tolerably good fliers. They seldom attempt to walk, and when sitting they bend their legs under them, and assume a very upright attitude.

The Eared Grebe is the rarest of the British species, and derives its name from a tuft of rich golden feathers which arise behind the eye of the adult bird. It is not nearly so large as the preceding species, being only one foot in length, and it may be distinguished from the young crested Grebe by the slight upward curve of the bill, and the absence of rusty red feathers between the eye and base of the beak.

The odd little PUFFIN, so common on our coasts, is remarkable for the singular shape, enormous size, and light colours of its beak, which really looks as if it had been originally made for some much larger bird. Owing to the dimensions of the beak it is often called the SEA-PARROT, or the COULTERNEB.

The Puffin can fly rapidly and walk tolerably, but it dives and swims supremely well, chasing fish in the water, and often bringing out a whole row of sprats at a time ranged along the side of its bill, all the heads being within the mouth and the tails dangling outside.

It breeds upon the rocks and in the rabbit-warrens near the sea, finding the ready-made burrows of the rabbit very convenient for the reception of its eggs, and fighting with the owner for the possession of the burrows.

Where rabbits do not exist, the Puffin digs its own burrow, and works hard at its labour. The egg is generally placed several feet within the holes, and the parents defend it vigorously. Even the Raven makes little of an attack, for the Puffin gripes his foe as he best can, and tries to tumble into the sea, where the raven is soon drowned, and the little champion returns home in triumph.

The egg is white, but soon becomes stained by the earth. The food of this bird consists of fish, crustaceans, and insects.

The length of this bird is about one foot.

PUFFIN.—*Fratercula Arctica.*

KING PENGUIN.—*Aptenodytes Pennanti.*

The Penguins form a very remarkable group, all its members having their wings modified into paddles, useless for flight, but capable of being employed as fore-legs in terrestrial progression when the bird is in a hurry, and probably as oars or paddles in the water. There are many species of Penguins, but as they are very similar in general habits, we must be content with a single example.

The King Penguin is a native of high southern latitudes, and is very plentiful in the spots which it frequents. It swims and dives wonderfully well, and feeds largely on cuttle-fish. Dr. Bennett has given an admirable description of this bird and its habits, as it appeared on Macquarrie's Island in the South Pacific Ocean.

"The number of Penguins collected together in this spot is immense, but it would be almost impossible to guess at it with any near approach to truth, as during the whole of the day and night thirty or forty thousand of them are continually landing, and an equal number going to sea. The females hatch their eggs by keeping them close between their thighs; and if approached during the time of incubation, move away, carrying their eggs with them. At this time the male bird goes to sea and collects food for the female, which becomes very fat. After the young is hatched, both parents go to sea, and bring back food for it; it soon becomes so fat as scarcely to be able to walk, the old birds getting very thin."

There is only a single egg, and its colour is greyish white.

WANDERING ALBATROS.—*Diomedéa éxulans.*

The Wandering Albatros is possessed of wondrous powers of wing, sailing along for days together without requiring rest, and hardly ever flapping its wings, merely swaying itself easily from side to side with extended pinions. Sometimes the bird does bend the last joint, but apparently merely for the purpose of checking its progress, like a ship backing her topsails. It is found in the Southern seas, and is very familiar to all those that have voyaged through that portion of the ocean. Like the petrel, it follows the ships for the sake of obtaining food, and so voracious is the bird that it has been observed to dash at a piece of blubber weighing between three and four pounds, and gulp it down entire. After this dainty morsel, the bird was not able to rise from the water, but yet swam vigorously after another piece of blubber on a hook, snapped at it and was only saved from capture by the hook breaking in its mouth.

SKUA GULL.—*Stercorarius catarrhactes.*
COMMON GULL.—*Larus canus.*
BLACK-BACKED GULL.—*Larus maximus.*
KITTIWAKE GULL.—*Ris*a *tridactyla.*

BRITISH GULLS.

The Skua is a large, fierce, and powerful bird, tyrannizing in a shameful manner over its weaker relations, and robbing them without mercy. It feeds mostly on fish, but prefers taking advantage of the labours of others to working honestly for its own living. As the lesser Gulls are busily fishing, the Skuas hover about the spot, and as soon as a poor Gull has caught a fish, and is going off to his family, down comes the Skua upon him with threatening beak and rushing wings, and when the victim drops his burden, to escape with greater facility, the Skua darts after the falling fish, and snaps it up before it reaches the water. It also eats eggs and the smaller birds, a propensity which is shared by other Gulls than the Skua.

The common Gull is too familiar to need much description, as it is well known to all who have visited the seashore, or the mouth of any of our larger rivers. It is a bold bird, caring little for man, and even following a steamer so closely that the gleam of its eyes can be plainly seen. It can easily be tamed, and is a rather useful bird in a garden, destroying vermin of various kinds, and occasionally killing and eating any small bird that may incautiously venture within reach of the strong bill. Cheese seems to be an acknowledged dainty with these birds, which have often been known to contract so great an affection for the place of their captivity as to return to it voluntarily, and even to introduce a mate to the well-remembered hospitalities.

The Great Black-backed Gull is a very fine bird, not very plentiful on our coasts, but spread over the greater part of the British shores.

This bird prefers low-lying and marshy lands, and is found on the flat shores of Kent and Essex at the mouth of the Thames, where it is popularly known under the name of the Cob. It is very plentiful on the shores of Sweden and Norway, and on some of the islands of Shetland and Orkney it breeds in abundance, the eggs being highly valued on account of their rich flavour and their large size.

The pretty Kittiwake Gull is tolerably plentiful on many of our shores, and breeds upon the rocky portions of the coast. Owing to the diversity of its plumage according to the age, the Kittiwake has been called by several names; "Tarrock" being the best known and belonging to the bird while young. The name of the Kittiwake is given in allusion to its cry, which bears some resemblance to that word rather slowly pronounced. The nest of the Kittiwake is made of seaweed, and placed on narrow ledges of rock at a great elevation. The nests are placed in close proximity to each other, and generally contain three eggs of a brownish olive, covered with spots of grey and brown.

The head and neck of the Kittiwake are white, the upper parts of the body silvery grey, the wings being diversified with a little black and much white. The under surface is pure white.

GANNET OR SOLAN GOOSE.—*Sula Bassánea.*

The Gannet, Solan Goose, or Spectacled Goose, is a well-known resident on our coasts, its chief home being the Bass Rock in the Frith of Forth, on which it congregates in vast numbers.

The Gannet is a large bird, nearly three feet long, and being powerful on the wing and possessed of large appetite, it makes great havoc among the fish which it devours. Herrings, pilchards, sprats, and similar fish, are a favourite food of the Gannet, and as soon as the shoals of herrings approach the coast, the Gannets assemble in flocks and indicate to the fishermen the presence and position of the fish.

The bird is able to catch its prey at some distance below the surface, and accomplishes its object by shooting directly downwards with partially closed wings and seizing the fish before it has time to take alarm.

The nest of the Gannet is a heap of grass, seaweed and similar substances.

CORMORANT.—*Gráculus Carbo*.

CRESTED CORMORANT.—*Gráculus cristátus*.

The common Cormorant is well-known for its voracious habits, its capacities of digestion having long become proverbial.

This bird is common on all our rocky coasts, where it may be seen sitting on some projecting ledge, or diving and swimming with great agility, and ever and anon returning to its resting-place on the rock. It is an admirable swimmer and a good diver, and chases fish with equal perseverance and success, both qualities being needful to satisfy the wants of its ever-craving maw. Eels are favourite morsels with the Cormorant, which, if the eel should be small, swallows it alive in spite of the writhings and struggling of its victim, and the many retrogressions which it will make from the interior of its devourer, until it is finally accommodated and digested, the latter being a process of wonderful celerity.

Another well-known British species of this genus is the Crested Cormorant, Green Cormorant, or Shag, a bird which can at once be distinguished from the preceding species by the green colour of the plumage and the difference in size.

PELICAN—*Pelecánus onocrótatus.*

We now arrive at the well-known Pelican.

This bird is found spread over many portions of Africa, Asia, and is also found in some parts of Southern Europe. It is a sociable bird, assembling in large flocks, and often mingling with the flamingoes, its white plumage contrasting finely with the scarlet raiment of its long-necked allies. The wings of the Pelican are very long and powerful, and the flight is singularly bold and graceful.

The colour of the Pelican is white with a delicate roseate tinge like that of a blush rose. On the breast the feathers are elongated and of a golden yellow. The quill-feathers are black, but hardly seen until the bird expands its wings.

DALZIEL BROTHERS, CAMDEN PRESS.

www.ingramcontent.com/pod-product-compliance
Lightning Source LLC
Chambersburg PA
CBHW032222230426
43666CB00033B/588